BEACON
OF THE
DARK NIGHT

ISBN: 979-8-3303-6914-0 (Paperback)
ISBN: 979-8-3303-7003-0 (ebook)

Library of Congress Control Number: 2024917892
Print: United States of America
Book Editor: Ceara Nobles
Cover Designer: Tatiana Vila
Interior Designer: Marta Dec

Social media platform handle: @DarkNightBeacon
Inquires: darknightbeacon@gmail.com

Beacon of the Dark Night:

Shining hope through the shadows

Dark Night Beacon

TABLE OF CONTENTS

CHAPTER 4: LOVE   143

AUTHOR BIOGRAPHY

Written under the pseudonym Dark Night Beacon, this book provides powerful quotes and captions for self-improvement. In its pages, you will encounter stories of resilience, tales of overcoming adversity, and profound reflections on the human spirit.

When he is not writing, the author spends his time reading, hiking, traveling, watching sports, spending time with family, and working as a law enforcement professional. His eloquent reflections have inspired countless readers to think deeply about their own lives and purpose.

A graduate from California State University, he obtained a Bachelor of Science degree in Criminal Justice with an emphasis on psychology and sociology. He's proficient in many studies, including cognitive behavior therapy, attachment, neuroplasticity, loss aversion, cognitive biases, social learning, transactional analysis, and psychosocial development.

He has many years of experience in mindfulness-based resilience training, trauma-informed responses, motivational theory, and receptivity. Throughout his career in law enforcement, he's gained valuable insights and stories of resilience, courage, and perseverance. He's learned life lessons such as leadership, handling pressure, and staying calm in crisis situations. It gives him natural authority on topics related to discipline, integrity, and dealing with tough situations, especially throughout his time as an instructor. He speaks more than one language fluently.

His unique experiences have been adapted into a motivational tool for handling personal crises. His purpose-driven style of writing aims to help others improve their lives. He writes with the reader's best interests in mind, because even the toughest circumstances can lead to personal growth and success. He has over ten years of writing experience and his work can be found on multiple social media platforms with unique followers from around the world under the username @DarkNightBeacon.

PREFACE

Inspired by my life's journey and the transformative circumstances I have faced, this book is for readers who have experienced loss, violence, personal vulnerability, emotional feud, and the struggle to rise above adversity. "Beacon" refers to a source of guidance, inspiration, or hope, while "dark night" is a period of personal difficulty, despair, or confusion. Like the gleam of a lighthouse, a beacon illuminates the dark to lead the way from uncertainty and vacillation to guidance and positive transformation.

The chapters in this book cover diverse topics that include life's varied aspects of darkness, mystery, love, faith, and compassion. Ignited by fire and extinguished by passion, you will walk through life's struggles and be presented with a bold response to each challenge with captions for well-known quotes from around the world. I attempt to expand on each quote and compare them to life experiences to establish a connection with you, the reader.

Through the pages of this book, you will encounter stories of resilience, tales of overcoming adversity, and profound reflections on the human spirit. Each chapter is crafted to resonate with the depths of your soul and encourage you to look beyond the surface of your struggles to find the strength within. Unless you change your perspective, making real changes in your life can be difficult. With more than two hundred inspirational quotes from the brightest minds, this book will not only help you understand them on a deeper level but will also motivate you to apply them in your own life.

In the face of intellectual challenges, may you discover the power of your mind to generate innovative solutions and new perspectives. When confronted with violence and personal vulnerability, may you find the fortitude to embrace peace and self-compassion. In times of catastrophe, may you uncover hidden opportunities for growth and renewal.

This book is not just a collection of words. It is a beacon of hope and a guide for those navigating the tumultuous seas of life. It invites you to embark on a transformative journey, to seek out the lessons embedded in every experience, and to emerge stronger and more enlightened through faith in God. I urge you to seek therapy, converse with friends and family, and when these options are not available and you seek out additional guidance, let this book be your convoy.

As you delve into these narratives, remember that you are not alone. The path to self-betterment is a shared voyage, and each step you take contributes to a collective story of human perseverance and triumph. Let these pages be your companion, your mentor, and your friend as you strive to become the best version of yourself. May you find the inspiration to rise above, the wisdom to understand your true essence, and the courage to live a life of purpose and fulfillment. I hope you find comfort and stay inspired for years to come.

INTERLUDE

My story did not start when I was born. It did not begin until I was a vulnerable young boy who experienced the unimaginable. Scared, confused, and alone, I stumbled across a life-altering situation, and it taught me that one must not take their freedom for granted. In the pitch of darkness and frigid air, a cloud of uncertainty silhouetted my frightened soul.

Governed by a whirlwind of adrenaline, I attempted to run away. I was confronted by something truly horrifying. An unknown person snatched me. I saw the evil look in their eyes, a demonic soul described as a mischievous and cruel apparition, glaring and hateful. Their clutch was like a vice and my attempts to break free were met with immense resistance. After several minutes of arduous struggle, I broke free and ran off.

Was this person who attempted to abduct me real or a product of my young and terrified imagination? I may never know, but I returned to this moment of intense fright to establish an iron-clad inner determination never to let myself be overcome by fear again. I made a deliberate choice to become a survivor, a warrior in the truest sense, by seizing that petrifying feeling of dread and forging it into strength and courage. That young boy emerged as the person I am today, rising into the light, lifted by the power of a thousand words. And thus, the miracle transformation was complete.

Your story may also contain trauma, pain, struggle, and battles that have caused you distress and doubt, but I am here to assure you that any obstacle in life can be overcome. Your transformation is in the making. All you have to do is stay determined, never surrender, and allow yourself to be inspired by the words in this book. May hope find you through your shadows. May it discover you in the depths of sorrow. And may it give you strength where despair lingers.

PROLOGUE

We are all damaged in some way or another. A lot of ink has been spilled penning the perceptions that come into existence post childhood trauma. You roam the path life allotted you, seeking to survive by balancing an impossible scale.

We all have experienced trauma in our lifetimes. We tread this world trying to balance what life throws at us and decipher situations based on the dark experiences we endured. The wounds we carry will stay with us. But should our past situations define our present or our future? No, they must not, and this demands us to be stronger than ever to continue with our lives while carrying these wounds.

It is human nature to be distressed or traumatized by the appalling experiences in life. They spark several powerful and disturbing feelings within us, affecting our basic traits, capabilities, and decision making, thereby inflaming our fear. Beneath the burden of such overwhelming thoughts, it is natural to feel helpless. One's reaction to trauma, while it happens as well as shortly afterward, governs the pace of one's recovery. Having a coping strategy for such scenarios is the key. Learning something from the situation can help you recover from a traumatic event, but so can seeking support from friends, family, or a support group.

People go through disquieting experiences, some of which can be as horrid as domestic violence, abuse, a natural disaster, or a serious accident. No doubt, when a child is traumatized, an indelible stamp is etched within their spirit that grows like a dreadful cancer as the child grows and matures. It becomes part of who they are.

How will you navigate your world with the weight of uncertainty and trauma?

CHAPTER I

DARKNESS

We all need darkness in our soul-searching journey. We often bemoan the dark, lash out against our painful and unwanted circumstances. However, there is something about the darkness, the placidity of its hour, creating its own dialect and liberation, and in that terrifying susceptibility, we allow ourselves to become vulnerable yet brave enough to say things we'd never say in the light. I invite you to find peace and beauty in the dark, for many gifts and lessons await you. You will appreciate the miracles of the dark because they will guide you to your new transformation.

1. THE DARK NIGHT

> *"Though my soul may set in darkness, it will rise in perfect light. I have loved the stars too fondly to be fearful of the night."*

SARAH WILLIAMS

Do you find yourself feeling fearful of the dark? Sometimes we find ourselves looking up at the universe and seeing the stars in the night sky. We discover that the dark night is insignificant. Perhaps it's nothing to be fearful of. We may even find the darkness to be our savior or a kind of emotional support. Although the night might be frightening, it contains a hidden treasure, only seen by those who appreciate it or relate to it.

We all have trials and challenging times in our lives. Many times, these ordeals keep us from doing the things we love and aspiring to succeed. We all have lost a dear one in the past, a loss that has kept us from moving on. But what encourages us to finally do so is the realization that a loss, however deep it might be, does not have the strength to hold us back from looking forward to the future. These losses are what motivate us to keep moving forward.

We must have hope that even though we will experience bumps in the road, if we keep our priorities on the things we love, life will be beautiful. These trials make us stronger. We would never see the stars if it were not for the darkness. Just like the murk of the dusk, life too brings phases of glum. One must not be afraid of this darkness, as it is only temporary.

People may be hurt, taken advantage of, used and discarded. It is in the darkness that we recognize the strength of the light, and we only appreciate it because of the inky black that surrounds us. Upon the path where you encountered the wrongdoers, you must have also come across people who endure danger to help and guide and heal the broken.

Misfortunes happen, and sometimes they happen to you. But no matter how scary life gets, there are those who make it better. Emerging from hardship reflects a journey of resilience where the light you seek symbolizes clarity and renewal. You, too, can add your shine to the constellation. You have adored the heavenly cosmos too fondly to be fearful of the night.

2. THE BROKEN WORLD

*"The broken world waits in darkness
for the light that is you."*

L. R. KNOST

Do not be unnerved by the brokenness of the world. Broken things can be mended. Not with time, but with a positive intention. Love intentionally, extravagantly, and unconditionally. The feeling of love is not foreign to our hearts; it is our natural emotion, our natural state of being. It is the way we come into the world.

Have you ever wondered how hate, anger, and dismay build up? There are as many individual triggers to cause that darkness to flare up as there are people whose hearts are sad. The more people you talk to and listen to, the more you'll realize that each person has a shard of jagged glass representing their own pain that they keep in a secret part of their heart.

Some individuals vent their concealed pain, polish it up and exhibit it to others, perhaps to impart the knowledge to everyone that they too have sadness, anger, or frustration. They want to reveal a point of sorrow which they might view as their ticket into the world—a life where they will be accepted and treated fairly, without being judged.

Maybe it's their way of saying they belong here in this world of darkness too. Life doesn't need to remain that way. We can change, heal, and grow. Most importantly, we can uncover the reality of the love with which we entered the world. We can share that with others instead of our stabbing pain. The light we seek is our inner fire, a belief that we can and will overcome.

So, forgive and forget. You are the light in this murky world. With good intentions, one should not fear change or lack inspiration. We should have patience and take responsibility for our every action. Most importantly, we must have faith in our Creator that there is a plan for each of us. There is a reason why we go through difficult moments in our lives, because without these tests, life would have no meaning.

3. THE SHADOW

"Deep into the darkness peering, long I stood there wondering, fearing, doubting, dreaming dreams no mortals ever dared to dream before."

EDGAR ALLEN POE

Deep in the darkness stands a frightening shadow. An apparition glows in the dark, eliciting a sense of fear.

Lethal as the night sky, the breeze cuts through the cold air. To some, you are a dream; to others, you are a nightmare. Your presence cannot be comprehended. Your symbol cannot be defeated. Your shadow cannot be ignored.

People will wonder about you while your enemies will doubt you. Your companions will question you while your acquaintances will fear you. Your supporters will be confused. Your adversaries will threaten you. Your rivals will be uncertain. Your opponents will not believe in you. Your nemesis will be suspicious. Your associates will be skeptical. Your allies will be wavering. But has it ever crossed your mind that it doesn't matter what others think of you? Your greatness will overcome it all.

These are the reasons for your motivation in life. In the end, nobody matters when you reach your destination. Other's opinions will fall short when you accomplish what your heart desires. You will be unstoppable. When you reach this level of confidence and credence, you will realize your true mental power. You will grasp your utmost intelligence and capabilities and use them to benefit your trek to glory and surpass your dreams.

Continue to dream the impossible and persevere in the tasks that others fail to accomplish or avoid. Each step forward is a testament to your courage and the unbreakable spirit within you. The idea of aspiring for extraordinary achievement and pushing beyond conventional limits despite the odds is the beginning of a transformative dream. Only then will you realize your true potential.

4. RETURN OF THE DARK

"May the darkness never leave me alone, for it is my strength. It's my armor. And to the darkness I shall return."

DARK NIGHT BEACON

May the darkness you feel, and witness forever give you strength. May it forever fuel your fire to keep going, to never give up. May the darkness consume you like the abyss. May the dark night power your soul and give you powers you never thought you were capable of. May gloom never abandon you, for its presence provides nourishment. May the twilight always follow you, dispensing you the courage you need.

I always feared the darkness, the shadows of my life. But I also relished its dark forces, the ones that kept me up at night. Darkness was bestowed upon me and that alone gives me the confidence to walk the storms of my life without hesitation. I discovered that darkness is nothing to be feared but rather to be embraced. I know that within the pitch of the dark, there awaits a plethora of beauty, gifts, and lessons. And that's how the dark became my peace, my beliefs, and the values that many feared from the unknown. It's a place I often visit, consciously and unconsciously, and will return to.

Although my passion for solitude will always remain strong, my desire for the dark to accompany me will always be greater. Only darkness can keep me safe; only its mysterious glow can protect my soul. It is where my life began and where it shall end. You too can utilize the power of darkness as a source of strength. You too can confront your deepest fears, pain, and insecurities by learning about yourself in ways the light doesn't reveal.

5. THE LIGHT OF DARKNESS

*"Darkness became your sunshine for you
had learnt to live in the shadows."*

SYEDA AMMARAH NAZAM

Darkness wears its own sheath of light. The chaos surrounding the mysteries of the dark is like a magnet that pushes you further into those depths. Eventually, the shadow becomes your best friend, your salvation. Love is about observing light inside the person who knows nothing but darkness. In my fatalistic moments, I have trouble comprehending the chaos in my mind and its tendencies. My weaknesses, the vulnerable side of me, remain concealed from the world.

For these reasons and many more, a part of me yearns to live in the shadows. I want to be understood. Maybe I am waiting to be brought to light like an illusion that materializes from darkness. Whatever it may be, I am willing to take that risk, knowing that it may destroy me. I have learned to cope with adversity and build resilience in the face of hardship. Living in the shadows means developing the strength and skills to navigate tough times.

The world is becoming more unpredictable, unsafe, and dangerous. I want to be saved from all the uncertainties of the world and be remembered for something meaningful. There is too much peril, too many hazards, and far too much unease in this life, so I patiently wait in the dark to finally be seen. It is time to shine the light within and seek the rewards hidden in the shadows to be victorious in any given moment.

I want you to believe that darkness can teach you the value of light. By enduring difficulty, you can develop gratitude for the brighter moments. The strength you gain isn't just about survival but about transforming pain into power. Thus, you emerge not only unbroken but stronger and more whole than before. The shadows help you navigate uncertainty by becoming adaptable and unafraid of the unknown.

6. DARKNESS AND FIRE

"We dare not talk of the darkness for fear it will infect us. We dare not talk of the fire for fear it will destroy us."

LUCY H. PEARCE

Fire fuels our prayers. We live and breathe like those before us. We come to the fire and feel it on our skin, in our hearts, and shining out through our eyes. Darkness, like fire, can consume us. Fire, like darkness, can destroy us. However, both darkness and fire can sustain us. They can give us power we never thought we were capable of.

Life can be truly enigmatic with its share of bewilderment and perplexities. Not everyone will understand you, nor will everyone appreciate you. If you wish to rise from darkness, you must first burn. You must walk through fire to endure the pitch black of darkness. Some live with a fire in their skin but a chaotic storm of darkness in their soul. Some prefer to be in the darkness, but their veins circulate fire. The truth is that darkness and fire motivate us all. Some of us are more capable of utilizing these unique inner powers than others.

Together, darkness and fire can create a powerful metaphor for inspiration. The combination can teach you that even when external circumstances are bleak, the potential for transformation and growth lies within you. Live in the depth of darkness and fire. Fear it, appreciate it, because you too will one day know how these intense elements fuel your soul to bigger and better things. Believe in yourself and your fire within. Let your passion rage like a forest fire as it engulfs the darkness of the universe.

7. THE ABYSS

"Looking at the abyss, you see the reflection of your soul. Without a blink, you stare at it. You are unfathomable. You are deeper than the abyss."

UNKNOWN

The abyss is a vast chasm. It's daunting for most people to peek into, because it is seemingly bottomless. If it looks back at you and you blink, it signifies that you're terrified the infinite space may engulf you and you might get lost. The abyss is a deep, immeasurable space that can portray time, a foe, a challenge, an obstacle, or anything that requires concentration and preparation to conquer.

Even with this frightening thought, I don't blink. I am fearless. I am deeper than the abyss. I am inscrutable and my soul is immeasurable. With incomprehensible thoughts and in an enigmatic state, my image turns obscure. The challenges life throws at me are just a test. These provocations are an opportunity to learn and improve myself. This is the type of confidence I want to instill in you.

Once you break your fear of this void, you become keen. You become perceptive in the way you walk and talk. Your thoughts become assertive. Your moods become convinced. Your work becomes composed. When the time arrives and everything you do is unperturbed, you'll know you have accomplished your goal. You will no longer care for negativity, and you will certainly no longer care about canards. When we become confident in our capabilities, nothing can stop us. It all starts by recognizing and looking into our own darkness and acknowledging the things we are not proud of and that need improvement.

8. THE DEEP DARK

"I have seen so much of the deep dark. How can I now crave to stand in the light?"

DARK NIGHT BEACON

I have observed the unseen. I have heard what no one has discerned. I have felt what cannot be made out. I have sensed the unperceived. How can I go through life after what I have been through? How can I overcome that traumatic experience? How can I move forward knowing that evil is everywhere?

Many of us have gone through challenges in life. We have all experienced obstacles and suffered setbacks. We have all stumbled and had difficulty and complications. Some of us fail to move forward because we allow ourselves to dwell upon negative thoughts. We must recognize that God does what He wills for reasons that are only known to Him. Any attempt to comprehend His wisdom with our limited minds, or to understand how our current situation fits in with His overall plan, can lead us to erroneous conclusions.

We must successfully maneuver through these barriers, learning the lessons needed to achieve our goals. We must not fear change or lack of inspiration. We must have patience and take responsibility. Most importantly, we must have faith in the Lord that there is an underlining plan for us. There is a reason we go through dark moments in our lives, and it is only through these experiences that we can appreciate the light.

9. OLD FRIEND

"Hello, darkness, my old friend. I've come to talk to you again."

PAUL SIMON

Do you find darkness to be a trusted companion? I remember my first descent into the dark feeling like I was drowning. I was blinded and lost. But as the days began to shorten, the moon started to shine more often. I found that darkness would rise on me, crest for a moment, then come crashing down and pull all beneath its rip. I found myself in havoc and thought I might not make it. I began to doubt myself. But as the night passed and the daylight revealed itself, I was gripped by loneliness. The light brought warmth and searing beauty, but it also brought inevitability.

As the aloneness began to take control, the night brought nightmares and threats to my soul. But the night also brought the promise of affection. It brought the feeling of significance. I made the effort to get closer. The night began to cast its shadow upon my soul and, in doing so, it became a trusted friend. I realized the night provided me with hope, and I began to speak to it, knowing my words would be safe.

Some of us feel comfortable in the dark. It brings us peace and calm. Darkness becomes our companion. We talk to the dark to free ourselves from fear. I can tell you there is nothing more profound than the dark, nothing more gratifying, because it's the moment we identify our true congruence and purpose in life.

10. THE FOREST

"I am a forest, and a night of dark trees. But the one who is not afraid of my darkness will find banks full of roses under my cypress."

FRIEDRICH NIETZSCHE

I am so detailed that others see me as a perfectionist. I always want to be thorough in whatever I do. However, perfectionism has everything to do with vulnerability. I fear that allowing for imperfection will result in failure. Many of us perceive embracing our flaws as giving up. We might tell ourselves that allowing someone else to really see us could lead to rejection. But perhaps there is more to it than always being complete.

Does your name have some connotation to the willow lands? This is a thick brush or forest that thrives in dark, foggy jungles. Do you find resemblance between your personality and the trees? You have a mysterious aura engulfing your persona. Don't be petrified by your ambience or startled by your vibe. The forest can teach us about vulnerability and relationships. Within the woodlands reside creatures, many of whom are hidden in uncharted dark spaces. The forest contains shadows and trails that lead to unseen destinations. There are also clearings, brooks, and flowers in the forest. One might hear birdsong or come upon a majestic view. You could avoid the forest to stay safe and avoid getting lost, but at what cost?

Like the darkness of a forest, I fear that secret place within myself that I see as unsafe, impenetrable, and unlovable. I avoid looking altogether by disguising or suppressing myself or leaving my true self buried somewhere within. Is this why I am so closed off to others? I similarly resist vulnerability in relationships. I hold myself back and close myself off. Allowing others in the forbidden spaces within myself leaves me vulnerable. Is this why I prefer to be alone?

As with the forest, entering that uncertain territory holds risks and uncertainties that are followed by abundant rewards. Only when we stop hiding can we truly know ourselves. When we are vulnerable to others, we can also find true connections. Only then can we reveal the good within us and appreciate the good in others.

11. THE ANOINTED

"I didn't choose darkness. Darkness chose me."

THE DARK KNIGHT

I didn't choose to stay in the dark. I did not pick my fate, nor did I relish my constant need to be just. I was chosen from the darkness, a place no one has ever been to before. I was raised from the cold, dark earth to keep the peace and so I learned to love the dark and assimilate with it.

We have learned to do the same in our own interior worlds. We fear the darkness, the shadows of our lives. We don't want to be still and sit in the silent night of our fears, terror, and our shame and regrets. We all make mistakes that we're not proud of, but these downfalls are as much a part of our human birthright as our existence and our ability to draw meaning from life. We would do almost anything to not have to spend time in the darkness of our souls.

The shadows in our world can become overwhelming and consume us. Those moments we're not proud of can alter our minds. Those memories we fear can bring grief and eclipses upon us. Those dark thoughts of despair we've had in the past can bring doubt to our capabilities. Those times when we have failed ourselves can lead to failure in other aspects of our lives. All of those are equally a part of who we are, like the medals we've won, the promotions we've received, and the love we have shared. And it is only when we can learn to love the beauty of the darkness that we can be fully alive and centered in our light.

12. THE UNKNOWN

"There is more to me than meets the eye. Stop trying to figure me out. I am beyond your understanding. I don't want to be known."

DARK NIGHT BEACON

My mysterious aurora is always hidden. I choose to remain unsolved. I travel in the dark when visibility is at its weakest. I am more than a mediator. My heart is stronger than a thousand flying bats, soaring to great heights. My power is always underestimated. I can never be understood. Many have tried to solve my riddle, but all have failed. When darkness falls on the cold aching night, it is I that reign over the night sky. This is the type of credence I want you to possess.

For most of us, situations are often not as simple as they seem to be. They can be puzzling, just like our complex personalities. We want to be composed, intelligent, self-confident, not grabbing attention from all corners of the world. To exude the mysteries of ourselves, we must first be confident and true to who we are. Self-confidence allows us to stand calm and secure, knowing that we have the strength of spirit and wisdom to handle life.

Some of us do not want to be known. As much as others try to get close, we are not eager to open or reveal ourselves. Respect those who choose not to be deciphered, for they have a reason that has strengthened their mistrust. Their suspicion, distrust, wariness, and doubt has surfaced from something, and only they are able to control these thoughts. Have patience, because those who remain hidden have the best stories to share and can very well be the one your heart has always desired.

13. THE DARK SIDE

"Everybody's got a dark side."

JOKER

They just wouldn't understand. I have this dark side that I can't really talk about or let out. There's a place that only I know; it's not pretty and few have ever gone there. If I show it to them now, will they run away? In my younger years, it seemed everyone had a dark side. I had this fear of letting my dark side out too much and letting too many people into it. But no one ever told me this feeling would extend into adulthood.

Our dark sides can permeate everything we do. I can recognize that people around me, no matter what age, are still struggling with elements of their dark side. Some of it stems from their younger years and has morphed and mutated over their entire lives. Some people develop a dark side in their adult years due to trauma.

Do we ever move beyond our dark side, or will there always be some form of it within us? No matter who you are or what your place is in life, you are likely wrestling internally with something that you hope other people won't discover about you. Dealing with your dark side requires an individual response, but you are not alone. We are all in the same struggle, each finding our way. Remember one important thing: you are not your struggle. Your dark side is not your identity. You are much bigger than that. Take the first step and start by letting someone know you care.

14. FEARLESS

"In the darkest moments, wait with no fear."

RUMI

How do we learn to revere the night and overcome our fear of it? Darkness provides a poetic mood that gives depth to the adventure of humanity. Without it, religious emotion vanishes, taking the identity of humankind and its culture.

'Darkest moments' can be defined as situations that can cause us harm. Many times, our inner voice can be a barrier that keeps us stuck. Other times, it's our psychological state that keeps us from getting what we want and becoming who we want to be. Learning to handle fear and overcome it is not a sample task.

When the darkest night approaches, have no fear. But understand it's the fear that gives life the thrill to live. Fear doesn't negate courage. It beckons it. Remember that fear itself isn't a problem. Our reaction to fear is the issue. In making fear an adversary, we miss the challenge of deciphering the message being sent to us. When we choose to make it an ally, we gain so much more. Fear and risk are vital components because that's when you start to come up with creative and interesting ways to survive and develop.

Patience is a quality that makes us stronger. It allows us to think before we act, thus minimizing mistakes. It allows us to fully comprehend a situation. It makes us calm, more alert and understanding. Remember that the beginning of wisdom is to conquer fear. Your experience will play a significant role in those defining moments when the dark hours roll down from the sky like a thick fog to blind your vision. Be brave. Ignore tomorrow, for you have seen yesterday and you are living the present moment today.

15. THE SERVANT

> *"You belong only to the night; outsiders are forbidden to infiltrate your heart. Only the cold, aching darkness is privileged to know your identity."*

DARK NIGHT BEACON

I hide my shadowed soul inside, seen through my dark, mesmerizing eyes. I keep a close eye from afar, making sure those I love are safe. But deep within my soul, I know that I belong to the night, a sphere where outsiders are forbidden to infiltrate my heart. Only the cold, aching darkness is privileged to know my identity.

Most people see the cold and sometimes arrogant and prideful side of me instead of the kind and compassionate person I truly am. I can appear cold and aloof toward others who wish to get close, but I'd rather be alone because I'll eventually get hurt when I lose my loved ones. I have been identified by a rare group of individuals. My calculated maneuvers are completed with perfect precision. My heart is full of passion and fire, yet it's in those moments of extreme rage that I can be vulnerable. It is then that my true caring heart can be deciphered.

My heart is sealed. No one can get close to me, not even those I love. A select few may get to know me, but I always find a way to push them away. My identity may never be known because I am the night, and only darkness can comprehend my soul. Darkness is my master, and I am its scion.

Keeping a low profile and maintaining a level of anonymity can offer various benefits. If you also choose to remain unknown, you allow yourself to live without the constant pressures of meeting societal expectations. You strengthen your decision making by basing it on personal values rather than external influences. You provide yourself with space to explore different aspects of your identity and the freedom to change paths without being judged by others. Choosing a life away from the spotlight is a choice that can lead to a more balanced and fulfilling life.

16. THE SHADOW

"Shadows speak louder than words."

TAY JEFFERIES HASSAN

A silhouette is the image of an object or scene represented as a solid shape of a single color, usually black, with its edges matching the outline of the subject. It describes the sight or representation of a person, object, or scene that is backlit and appears dark against a lighter background. Silhouettes are elegant and seemingly magical. They are a common artistic device as they occur organically in our natural surroundings. That's what I want you be: A silhouette, rarely seen and yet believed by many.

Against the sky, the stars crown you, marking the edges of your silhouette like you are a constellation yourself.

Although shadows can be difficult to see, their presence can be felt. They may not be heard, but they can be perceived. Use your mind and heart to show affection, attention, and awareness. Be alert to unseen feelings and manifest the unheard care because only you can bring positivity through the cloud of uncertainty when words are not enough. Impressions and evidence left behind by actions can have a greater impact than mere words.

Life consists of rare, isolated moments of the greatest significance, and of innumerable intervals during which, at best, the silhouettes of those moments hover about us. Seeming utterly fragile and vulnerable, the silhouette pulses almost imperceptibly with the beating of your heart as if you are whispering soundless words to the darkness.

17. THE DARK LIFE

"And not every time when the sun rises do we all feel alive. For some, darkness is life."

DARK NIGHT BEACON

I have a dark soul, an enigmatic individual who seems to battle as much with myself as I do with the world around me. Darkness is my life in a nutshell. There is something inherently fascinating about the dark, about the more morally ambiguous parts of life. It is an organic attraction, for we are made of light, dark, and everything in between.

Some of us spend most of our lives reconciling the seemingly disparate fragments that shape us and our identities, including interacting with and making peace with our dark sides. It comes as no surprise, therefore, that we connect with fictional characters who undergo similar journeys. The archetypal hero's journey throughout world mythology in all forms and interpretations details their experiences through considerable trauma, danger, and shadows.

As writers, readers, artists, and audience members, we engage with these characters. We undergo their cathartic journey, which puts us in touch with parts of our own selves and our society. We often face struggles like the characters who rise above difficult circumstances. Their journey can inspire us to confront our own challenges with a similar mindset. It is this reason why I always considered Batman my childhood hero. You too can find meaning in a fictional character that will resonate with your soul. They will serve as powerful reminders that, just like them, you can grow, persevere, and overcome whatever challenges come your way.

18. UNCERTAINTY

"Fear of the unknown is the greatest fear of all."

YVON CHOUINARD

Uncertainty is part of the human experience. Some thrive in uncertain times; others become emotionally paralyzed. The way people respond to uncertainty may depend on how afraid they are of the unknown. If you fear spiders, it's based on what you've learned—some of these arachnids are venomous and deadly, while most are harmless. But not all fears are based on such concrete information.

Some fears are based on what you don't know. Entering an unknown cave can be thrilling but also frightening. You don't know what is beyond the darkness. You don't know how far your imagination may take you. A more personal example? The fear of public speaking. Part of the terror many people feel onstage is not knowing how the audience will respond.

Fear of the unknown is a basic part of many other anxieties, fears, and phobias. You don't know what you don't know. For example, if you don't know how big and mysterious the universe is, you can't be afraid of it. But once you are made aware there is a lot out there that you don't understand, it suddenly becomes scary to know what you don't know.

Experience the unknown, the dark side of the world. Discover the mysteries of the human mind. Find the meaning of the puzzles that haunt you. Become the riddle yourself. Create a puzzle to astonish others. Once you experience real fear, you'll understand your true self in ways you never have before.

19. INFATUATION FOR THE DARK

"My love for darkness and the night will never end, as it is the only time when I can unveil my mask and be myself."

DARK NIGHT BEACON

Have you ever experienced negative darkness, those long stretches of the night when you can't sleep and worry about everything? The night's murkiness can sometimes seem interminably long, compared with daytime. However, this slowing of time can be the most relaxing and beautiful experience. Some fear this moment and a rare few relish in its addictive beauty. The tranquil dark can be beautiful too.

Growing up, we learned to think about the dilemmas we couldn't solve. We mastered the importance of dream time and its correlation to human wellbeing. The night allows this dream time, and the heavier, thicker dark of winter gives us a chance to dream a little more while we are awake. This kind of reverie and meditation can slow the constellation and provide a silence in the darkness that sits under the winter stars.

I always enjoyed the dark. I have a profound interest in the stillness of the night. Darkness is my savior. It is the only time I can be who I really am. It allows me to feel my smartest, most creative, and most productive in the evening or night hours. It lets me reveal who I really am and my purpose in life. In the darkness, I can accomplish all my goals. My identity is revealed, and not many individuals know of my true self. But when will I disclose my dark side to those who are intrigued? What you seek hides not in the light, but in the shadow it casts.

20. STILLNESS

"There's something about the darkness, the stillness of the hour."

TAHEREH MAFI

We need darkness in our soul-making journey through life. There are treasures hidden in our hearts, treasures we ourselves do not know of, though we may sometimes get a glimpse of the riches within. More often, we lament the dark, lash out against our unfortunate circumstances, and ignore sparks of light that flicker in the cosmos.

There's something about the dark, the serenity of the moment, that creates its own language. There's a strange kind of salvation in the dark, a terrifying vulnerability that we experience at exactly the wrong time, tricked by the darkness into thinking it will keep our secrets. The nurturing power of darkness is a great gift from God. But how hard is it for us to believe this?

How difficult to wait with patience, with acceptance, for the creative power of God to bring us through? For those who live in a land as dark as death, a light has dawned. Dark times evoke a sense of quiet and calmness to fill the night. It allows a peaceful, reflective, and introspective moment to be able to contemplate life in a meaningful manner.

Seasons of growth take time. No one becomes fully human in an instant. In calm detachment lies your safety, your strength in quiet trust. We do not lose hope in the darkness, nor do we give up the struggle. We trust as we reach out to, and work with, our compassionate Creator. We can be certain that, no matter how terrible our lives may seem, God will, in His own time, fill us with light. Then our life, like the raindrop, will reflect something of His beauty. We forget that the blackness is not a cloak, that the moon will soon rise. But in the moment, at least, we feel brave enough to say things we'd never say in the light.

21. MASTERPIECE

> *"If you can't see the beauty in your darkness; if you don't think maybe you might be a little piece of magic; don't you dare say that you are just another person. Because you're a masterpiece."*

DARK NIGHT BEACON

Life never went easy on me, and I didn't go easy on myself either. I am strong and others can see it in my eyes. They can sense it in my voice. I believe that my body can rebuild and heal itself. I know what it is like to be under-appreciated. Believing in myself means having confidence in my own abilities. It means trusting myself to do what I say I'll do and knowing those efforts will result in the desired outcome.

Always have that confident mindset. Never allow negative thoughts to prevent you from reaching your goals. If you find yourself at a dead end, start over. Learn and grow to fight another day. You truly are unique and only you hold the key to your success. Embrace your imperfections, struggles, and vulnerabilities. Find value and growth in your dark experiences.

Are you beautiful because you know your own darkness and it doesn't stop you from finding your own light? The price is steep, but you will come to appreciate the things you discover while stumbling in the dark. By enduring darkness, you come to discover deeper compassion for others. You learn your limits and strengthen your boundaries. There are still places where darkness lurks, but it is less intimidating in the light.

See the beauty in your darkness. Be proud of every aspect of your being. You are magical, just the way your

Lord created you. But most importantly, you are loved. When the night arrives and you comprehend your eminence, your obstacles will diminish, and your goals will be within reach. You cannot change a masterpiece because you are the living paragon. And that is why you are always thankful to God.

22. DEMONS

"Don't get too close; it's dark inside. It's where my demons hide."

IMAGINE DRAGONS

Are you aware of your dark side? Perhaps you observe your struggles with your demons, but do you want to hide your fiend? Or does your consciousness not allow you to do so? Maybe I'll eventually end up revealing my true thoughts and intentions. We all have flaws, and some of us put up walls to keep people out. I don't want them to get close; I believe it's too dark for them. I keep my feelings trapped inside and do not let them out. But when I pretend everything is fine, my misfortunes get worse.

Don't be afraid of the darkness. I know it can be difficult to push someone away for their own protection knowing they are also your salvation. But if they were the light of your life, then at some point they'll shine that light into your darkness. Share the beauty of your dark side. Allow it to resonate with others. Do the exact opposite and let others get close. Let them decide if they are too fearful of your darkness or brave enough to learn and develop their own unique dark side.

Everyone has secrets, and we often try to solve our problems alone. But when you see someone's eyes, you can observe their secret pain. We create our own world with our secrets, and it is very different from the real one. Address the dark side within you, the one you are not proud of, the one that convinces you that you have failed because of your past mistakes. Acknowledge them by bringing them to light instead of allowing them to pull you down.

23. LIGHT OF GOD

*"When the night comes, darkness
fulfills everything you see."*

DARK NIGHT BEACON

The idea of becoming spiritually weak can affect us all. There have been moments when even words eluded me, leaving me bereft of the capacity to express myself on paper. Unable to hear the message or articulate my thoughts, I sink into the dark night of my soul. I disappear like invisible ink.

I doubt anyone noticed. After all, it's safer to hide when I'm depressed, physically or spiritually, instead of asking for help or prayer. Why invite someone to judge me or tell me to "get over it" when there's already enough self-condemnation smothering my mind? Do you sometimes feel completely quiet? Are there times where you don't feel any emotions? You could laugh, chat with a friend, or text platitudes to the dark souls around you. A person must step close and gaze into the window of your soul to notice the flame that flickers and dims. They must listen, if only to hear the hum of your silence.

Sometimes it's impossible to explain the extent or depth of one's tragedy. Could you blame your dark night on unmet expectations or unconfessed sins? Could you attribute it to a deep disappointment or failure? What about your traumatic experiences in the past? Who knows what triggered the night. But when you've experienced holy companionship with the Lord, it's despairing to cry to God and hear nothing.

The longer my soul stayed in the dark, the less I prayed. At some point, prayer seemed worthless, giving rise to an inexplicable frustration and exhaustion. Telling the truth didn't get me anywhere. In fact, it made things worse. But one day, I stopped staring inward and gazed outward toward the Creator. I continued to pray. I bowed down to the great Almighty who cares for His beloved and longs for me to experience abundant life. I raised my silent voice to the Lord, who heals the soul and makes it new.

As darkness rained down upon me, a pinhole of light blasted into my dark soul. The longer I remained patient, the more brilliant His light shone within me until my dark night of mourning turned into a beautiful night. I realized my Guardian was with me the whole time. He was there for me every step of the way. And with that persistent faith in Him, I can sleep soundly, knowing that I am protected.

24. THE MAZE

*"I learned to love every part of me,
even the dark and twisted."*

SAMUEL DECKER THOMPSON

I'm terrified of the future, afraid that it will only hold more pain, more loss, more suffering. I don't know how many days it's been since I failed, and it doesn't concern me. But then I realize something is missing. I drag myself out of bed and look in the mirror. I look exactly how I feel. Suddenly, I realize that if I ever want to get back on my feet, I need to learn to love myself. But something is not right.

Learning to love ourselves is not so simple. We often believe we love ourselves, and yet our actions and reactions suggest otherwise. Loving ourselves is essential to our personal growth, to the fulfillment of our dreams, and to developing healthy, happy relationships with others. Instead of trying to talk to yourself into believing you have self-love, you must foster compassion for yourself. Even if you feel that deep down inside your soul, there is a void you cannot fill, you need to find a way to navigate the maze of unmet emotional needs, unresolved trauma and deep longing for meaning.

All these things help me to develop a sense of accomplishment, a sense of pride in what I am doing and who I am, and a realization that I am a worthy, talented, capable person who deserves to be loved. And the most important person to believe is me.

But then I remember that I've lost something, and I want it back. My journey isn't complete and never will be, but I have come a long way in my practice and hope to help others. You too can find beauty and hope even in the darkest moments through self-trust. Self-love is accepting yourself wholeheartedly and treating yourself with kindness. By setting boundaries and celebrating achievements, you can develop a healthy sense of self-worth.

The truth is, I liked being alone. I craved that time to wander through the endless maze of my own thoughts and daydreams. I made peace with myself long ago. I wanted nothing more. I felt complete and was content—at least until I became aware of the existence of the dark night.

25. HIDDEN LIGHT

"Don't fear the darkness; fear the shadow."

DARK NIGHT BEACON

You might find yourself asking, "What is the difference between darkness and shadow?" Darkness is the absence of light while shadow is the light hindered to give the shape of a silhouette. Darkness and light are both important in the rhythm of our lives. Life grows in the darkness. Hidden in the silent earth, seeds and bulbs are nurtured until the day comes when they emerge into the light.

We, too, need darkness in our journey of self-introspection. Hidden treasures are found in our hearts, treasures we ourselves do not know of. We may sometimes get a glimpse of the riches within, but more often they stay there unbeknownst to us. We lament the dark, lash out against our painful and unwanted circumstances, and ignore the little sparks climbing toward the light. Our unfortunate past creeps up during our darkness.

God has bestowed upon us the miracles of the dark. Within it, you will find aspects of yourself that are often seen as flaws or weaknesses. When you acknowledge the dark, you become fearless, and when you become fearless, you become relentless. With patience, you will see the light dawn upon your soul. This light will emit a provisional shadow, but the fear associated with it is short term. The dark will remain, and that's your opportunity to take the next step toward attainment.

Success takes time. You can't conquer your fears instantly. Do not lose hope in darkness. No matter how dark your life can be, the Lord will eventually illuminate your path. The shadows of your life are temporary. They will obscure your vision and blur your trace, but the dark will always reveal your goals and ambitions. You can be fearful of the shadow, but know that the dark will be your shield.

26. THE UNSEEN

"I have chosen to dwell in a place you cannot see."

RUMI

Choosing to remain unknown can mean a conscious decision to live a minimalist lifestyle or focusing on personal growth rather than seeking external validation. People will attempt to analyze me, and they will not know me because I am unique in the way they see me. If they place themselves in my shoes and see me as I see myself, they will see that I desire to reside in a place unseen.

Privacy is important to me. My focus is authenticity and personal safety. Choosing to limit my mystique is one way to avoid conforming to societal expectations. I want to lead a simple, unobtrusive life, and if anyone dares to draw near me or attempt to decode my charisma, they will always fail. People try to silence my allure and attempt to understand me. They try to approach my soul, but they stall. People make assumptions about me and adopt false ideas. They try to perceive me in what makes sense to them, but they do not know my true nature, demeanor, bearing, or manner.

When you choose to remain unknown, it will bother people. They will at some point stop trying to figure you out because you're beyond their understanding. When you are out of sight, your passions and desires are revealed. When your identity is obscured, your persona becomes published. There is great strength in the decision to remain in the dark. Being secluded requires self-confidence and the fortitude to endure hardship. When you choose to reside in darkness, that is when your soul is ready to attain glory.

27. THE REVELATION

> *"I embrace the darkness and confide with the shadows. I build walls around me to absorb the silence. I do not need anyone or rely on anything."*

DARK NIGHT BEACON

My appreciation for the dark is profound. The shadows reveal my identity. Silence is my weapon of choice. I push away those who choose to get near you. Like a shield, I block hearts that attempt to understand me and prefer the warmth of my cocoon. The risk is too great.

I do not rely on anyone. After all, I had to fend for myself during my traumatic situation. I called for help and no one answered. I begged for mercy and not a single soul came to my aid. I learned that within me is all that I need to be self-sufficient. Perhaps I am making a mistake by not relying on others.

We build walls around us to keep sadness out, but those same walls also keep out the joy. Sometimes we feel like we can do everything ourselves, and we are capable, but only to a certain extent. The journey to experiencing wholeness is fulfilled only when we bring others along for the ride. Lacking support, the solitary traveler soon becomes wary or fearful and is likely to quit. Finding our way involves clues that are subtle and sometimes misleading, requiring the kind of discernment that can often only happen in dialogue. We need other people to invite, amplify, and help discern life. This is how we can achieve completeness and solidity.

28. BLACKNESS

"I have said that black has it all. White too. Their beauty is absolute. It is the perfect harmony."

COCO CHANEL

Black is the only color that can stand alone and give other colors a certain depth. For this reason, many people appreciate its value. It evokes strong feelings that sometimes can be hard to explain. Black holds mysterious associations, yet it is a respectable color that holds much depth. Many consider it to be the most powerful color.

It's colorless yet contains all the colors at the same time. It has the power to command attention in any scenario. You could be an artist using black in paintings or simply throwing on a black jacket to elevate your look.

In color psychology, black represents anything but weakness. It's elegant, bold, confident, powerful, and sophisticated. It also gives off a mysterious nature that draws people in. Due to this symbolism, you'll notice that many luxury fashion houses embrace the use of black. Apart from the attractive nature of this color, black also has some negative connotations. People often associate it with death, sadness, fear, darkness, and despair. Without a doubt, the word 'black' holds significant power. It is beyond a simple color; it elicits emotion.

The dark doesn't attract attention, and that is perhaps what I prefer. The color black helps me hide in the dark, and darkness is my greatest advantage in being stealthy. The gloom provides me comfort. For these reasons and many more, I will always remain in the dark. I appreciate the color black because no other color can reproduce it, and no other color can defeat it. Remain undefeated in your life's battles as you conquer your destiny. Through the color of the dark, your soul can associate with the elegance and power of mystery. It can elicit a sense of self-confidence and display your importance to the vast world around you.

29. THE GAZE

"And if you gaze into the abyss, the abyss gazes also into you."

FRIEDRICH NIETZSCHE

When you look into the darkness, it stares back at you. The profound chasm tells you what you are made of. In the midst of monsters, you can find your own heroism and the goodness of others. It's a good thing to remember when you have experienced trauma. Maybe your abyss opened years ago, when your beautiful younger years fell apart. Maybe it crept into the phase of your life when you thought you had it all figured out. Or perhaps darkness enveloped your heart when you were abandoned.

It was years before I realized that what I endured was not only an experience, but a period of extreme transformation. An alteration, a revision of my soul through the journey of life. It was devastating for me. The terror of a mind that wasn't working the way that it should. I had to work from behind, trying to build a case, fighting to get myself out of the darkness that was slowly consuming me. I cycled up and down in mood and became so overmedicated that I could not put a sentence together.

I stared into that abyss and found that, as a person, I not only had voices, but the shadows were also present. Was it all a bad dream or a disowned part of myself? Was I trying to validate my existence? Was the unconscious depth of my being something I feared? When the abyss stares back at us, it stares at the feebleness of the conscious ego that thinks it can see, understand, or control our dark side. When the conscious ego stares at the archaic authentic self, the obsolete self stares back at the conscious ego. We realize that we carry more darkness in our souls than we care to admit.

The universe was cold and alone and asking me for answers just as much as I was asking it, and that was a terrifying revelation. It is a heavy burden when you realize you are something that anchors the nothingness, that sanity binds the insanity, that warmth secures the cold and substance fastens the void.

Don't be afraid to look into that abyss. You'll be amazed at how much strength you have.

30. ALONE

*"From childhood's hour I have not been, As others were.
I have not seen, As others saw.
I could not bring, My heart to joy at the same tone.
And all I lov'd—I lov'd alone"*

EDGAR ALLAN POE

I am unique. I was never able to fit in and found myself melancholy throughout my childhood. I was often left out. The subject of loss and unhappiness summarized my upbringing. I was not like the other children in my outlook, my play, my enjoyment. I knew I wasn't normal or happy like the others were. My joys were not the same and did not come from the same place.

I was always alone with my pleasure and love. The mystery that holds me together came from every experience I had. This formed my temperament and personality. During my childhood and in the beginning of my stormy life, I was a part of both the systole and diastole experiences. In some ways, I was protected by darkness, thunder and lightning. I was guarded by the precipice of danger, by the moon that encompassed me. I sometimes look back at my life and see the dark sky and heavens above; yet one of the clouds appear like the shape of a bat.

I realized my life will never be like the others. My time will never be spent the same way. It dawned on me that life was meant to be cruel to me. Why? Because I was chosen to be the one, the image that stands for peace and is characterized by love. And I would endure the pain all over again so that my loved ones could be content; so that my friends could be happy; so that the community I serve can be safer. I quietly love, and I secretly adore. Within my heart, I love alone, and it's this ultimate sacrifice that makes me stand above the rest.

If you felt markedly different from those around you at some point in your life, it means you experience things much more intensely and imaginatively than other people. While that can feel like a burden, it's also a source of identity, vision, and inspiration. It is your very nature to ask you who you are. The very thing that isolates you also makes you special. This isolation is part of being in contact with the extreme and mysterious dark depths of your soul, the very depths you need to become a writer.

CHAPTER II

SUCCESS

Experiencing an adventurous life is one way we can understand and appreciate our existence. We must live to write about life. The purpose of your journey is to be honorable, compassionate, and to leave a legacy of kindness. I share my travels and write about my experiences by exploring places that awaken my soul. Life analogies are used in this chapter to guide you to the path of discovery, adventure, and eagerness to move into the unknown. You will be motivated to learn about the depths of your own soul and draw parallels between everyday experiences and broad life concepts to convey a deeper meaning of life.

1. THE PURSUIT

"Many are stubborn in pursuit of the path they have chosen, few in pursuit of the goal."

FRIEDRICH NIETZSCHE

Setting a goal means putting expectations on yourself. It's about the destination, not the journey. We must always choose a goal with a challenging path. It's not unfavorable to get other people's perspective when you tell them you're about to follow your dreams. An outside opinion can provide some perspective, but we must know how to separate constructive criticism from negativity.

Too often, we allow distractions to get in the way of reaching our dreams. Even if your dreams fail, you'll feel proud you gave it your all to accomplish them. Dreamers fail now and then, but they also learn more in life. You learn from failure. The real world operates differently from the way we think and comprehend life. This dream path for some people may pan out, but for most of us, the road to our dreams is long, challenging, and unexpected. We should never choose the easy way out or a simplified path to destiny. Our noble course should be one where we are content with the challenges that come to us.

When you put full effort and exhaust all you have toward what you want, you will realize the true meaning of life. The experience of pursuing your dreams is often more rewarding and more enlightening than the achievement of your ambitions. Persistence is much of what separates the successful from the wishful thinkers. Distinguish yourself by staying motivated even in the toughest of circumstances.

The next time you feel challenged or disillusioned in the pursuit of your dreams, remember the ultimate destination. By adopting the perspectives of people who have already achieved their dreams, you can wrap your mind around the challenges you face in your own life and remain resolved in accomplishing your goals.

2. SHORTCUTS

"There are no shortcuts to any place worth going."

BEVERLY SILLS

In life, there are no quick and easy solutions. You must emphasize hard work, dedication, and face challenges head-on to achieve success. One of my experiences with attempting to find an easier path was when I hiked the Goat Canyon Trestle, the world's largest all-wood trestle. Built in 1933 with a length of 600 feet and standing 180 feet tall, it's an iconic hike through a meandering trail in the spectacular Carrizo Canyon, hidden miles away from civilization. There are no shortcuts to getting to the bridge and the direct route is through a desert land.

Although it doesn't offer a big mountain climb, it is a strenuous hike through a harsh desert environment, with over seven miles of distance to cover, not to mention a long drive on a dirt road to reach the trailhead. Hikers, historians, and desert enthusiasts across the world revere the historic engineering curiosity that stands in splendid remoteness in a rugged corner of Anza-Borrego Desert State Park. Finding a short route was ideal, given the difficult terrain, not to mention the time constraints. Unfortunately, I realized the only way to get to my destination was to hike the only route available. No shortcuts in sight.

This hike brought challenges of desert navigation and difficult terrain to accomplish the trek. It left me with the confidence that I can handle all kinds of situations in a dry, forbidding environment. You, too, can acknowledge life's difficulty and danger. Perhaps you trekked through an unforgiving desert landscape full of sand, rocks, and cacti, almost entirely exposed to the sun. Maybe you faced danger when none of your hike's routes were maintained and there were no official trails to follow. In addition to understanding desert navigation, you traversed big boulders and rocks and getting lost was a reality. Remember that there are no shortcuts in life; they only grease the rails to disappointing outcomes. May your journey in life always be safe and joyful. May achieving your goals require minimal effort, with ethical practices, and accelerate your soul growing journey.

3. DIFFICULTY

"Do not pray for an easy life. Pray for the strength to endure a difficult one."

BRUCE LEE

I certainly have not had an easy life. As a young child, I endured unimaginable loss, pain, trauma, and neglect. I battled inner demons and had the courage to withstand the impossible. Every challenge I faced gave me the strength to continue. Every grueling moment provided me with the courage to move forward. Each time, I prayed that I would be equipped with faith and determination to conquer my goals, aspirations, and to uncover my purpose in life.

We all face difficulty in life. Some of us will accept the challenge while others will be afraid to. Some of us will be thankful for these trials and tribulations, while others will wish for the nightmares to stop. When we have a clear understanding of why these things happen in our lives, we become believers. We begin to understand our path.

Few understand that all matters are in the hands of God. However, for some, their faith can be shaken during times of hardship. It is during those times, though, that we must remind ourselves that a believer's position and rank are raised in front of God. Our hardships may very well be a sign of God's love for us. This can help us in maintaining and even strengthening our faith.

Some of us believe that in all cases, trials can be good for the true believer. If we are tested with prosperity, we should remain grateful, and if we are tested with hardship, we should remain patient. We will receive a reward. We should not pray for an easy life with no challenges. We should pray for strength and the tenacity to endure hardship and come out stronger. An easy life is not fulfilling or a life worth living. Work to achieve a life that you can be proud of. Learn the valuable lessons and experience difficulty on your path to achieving greatness.

4. THE WATERFALL

"Life is like a waterfall. It's beautiful, yet harsh."
UNKNOWN

Over the years, I've completed many hikes along waterfalls, cascades, and chutes. Each one was unique in its own beauty and each one offered a special perspective on the route. The sight, visibility, panorama, outlook, and vista were always appreciated because, like life, they changed by the hour.

There is no better place to find yourself than standing by a waterfall and listening to its music. The roar of the falls is harsh and crashing. It silences the stream's peaceful song. At a certain time in your life, maybe you felt like the loud, harsh waterfall. In truth, life is like a waterfall. No matter how hard things get, it just keeps flowing forward.

There is undeniable beauty in a waterfall. What makes this continuously flowing body of water so majestic? Waterfalls are strikingly powerful; they are chaotic, roaring, and continuously in motion. Yet, as viewers, we perceive it as tranquil and hypnotizing. Why not view life as we view a waterfall? We all know life can get hectic. It can be formidable, and difficulty materializes often. The point of life is to embrace the challenges in this continuously changing, chaotic existence.

The waterfall is constantly diverted along its course. At each moment, these drops of water are pulled down by gravity, bouncing around with other drops of water and rocks, sticks, anything in the way. Yet at the end of every fall, there is a serene pool of placid harmony, an ebb waiting to flow.

As we continuously mature as human beings, there are those who remain static in their existence at a young age because of a distinct discomfort with the idea of change. And then there are those who prosper. It is our duty, as individuals in a constantly changing world, to continue to embrace change and accept it at a fundamental level.

Embrace every day and every hardship you encounter. There is tranquility at the end of every chaotic waterfall, there is calm after every storm, and there truly is a light at the end of every tunnel. There is a very human tranquility in change, so embrace every challenge and uneasy experience in your life. To do so is to grow as a human being and prosper into something far more beautiful than you could ever imagine.

5. SPELUNKING

"It begins when you pop your headlamp, illuminating the perpetual darkness of the abyss."

DARK NIGHT BEACON

Caving, also known as spelunking, is the extreme sport of exploring caves. The world has a vast number of caves, and most have not been explored. Caving is a physical sport and is not for those who are claustrophobic. Exploring a cave can be one of life's most exhilarating experiences. Crawl head-first into passageways so narrow they appear like little more than wormholes into the unknown, and you will start to understand what off-trail caving is about. One moment you're climbing a steep, muddy boulder, and the next you're slithering between cracks and marble, dragging yourself on knees and elbows.

Like life, you may feel alone and scared, but even in the darkest passageways, you can see the faint glow of light beckoning you home and promising success. Spelunking can be physically challenging, exhilarating, and certainly not for those with claustrophobia. Ducking into narrow tunnels and using fixed rope to descend steep drops can be very challenging. Like life, we face many obstacles, highs and lows, to be successful.

My first experience in cave exploration was at the Oregon Caves National Monument and Preserve. Deep within the Siskiyou Mountains are dark, twisting passages that awaited my discovery. It allowed me to experience something new around every corner. Each room had a secret waiting to be discovered. Each chamber had its own mystique.

Once I became comfortable, I turned off my headlamp and remained silent. Utter darkness overcame me, immensely deep and thick. It seemed almost tangible, like a substance you could touch. The strangest part of sitting in that level of darkness is I couldn't see my own body, not even my hand inches from my eyes. My mind would hover somewhere in the blackness, clinging to the sound of water dripping on rock. The feeling was both peaceful and disorienting, something I had never experienced anywhere else.

Being encased by stone hundreds of feet thick is a strange experience, and probably a good way to lose your mind. But it's also a way to connect with a part of earth that still feels primal and raw, and that can only be found while exploring caves. There's nothing more thrilling than the mystery of the unknown. If you open your heart and embrace it, you will change your life in unimaginable ways.

6. SWIMMING

"Water was something he loved, something he respected. He understood its beauty and its dangers."

BENJAMIN ALIRE SÁENZ

Swimming requires one's entire body to move through the water. It opens opportunities for other water-based activities such as rowing, sailing, and water skiing. Swimming provides a proving ground for some of the most fundamental and critical things that you will carry with you for the rest of your life. It has health benefits by keeping your heart and lungs healthy, improves strength and flexibility, and increases stamina, balance, and posture.

But besides these health benefits, swimming can also bring you success in life. Whether in your career, in personal relationships, or even different sports, swimming will teach you the importance of hard work, of being humble, and of being a team player. Accomplishing goals often requires giving what may seem like unnatural levels of effort.

Make working hard your talent and you will never go without success in the pool and in life. It won't always be fair, and things won't always go the way you plan. There will be times where no matter how hard you work; the results won't match your effort. You will get flustered as you get up on the blocks and totally choke. These moments sting, and they can drown you, but they also teach you how to be mentally tough, to overcome and to be humble, to rise above our challenges.

We might be tempted to succeed on our own, to say we did it with no help. But when you can corral the effort and the will of the group for a common goal, incredible things begin to happen. One swimmer chasing prominence is powerful, but a group chasing greatness is unstoppable.

Winning is great and losing is unpleasant, but the outcome matters more than anything else. You will lose many times over the course of your life. You don't have to like it, but being able to lean across the lane line and shake the winner's hand means that even though you didn't conquer the competition, you conquered yourself. Similarly, there will be triumphs and highs during your time in the pool. Being a champion is more than just being the first swimmer to the wall. It's being humble in victory, congratulatory to others, and setting an example for those to come.

7. ZIPLINING

> *"Life is like ziplining. It's over before you know it and you don't remember much because it all went too fast."*

LINDA POINDEXTER

A zipline is a pulley suspended on a cable and mounted on a slope. It enables a person attached to the pulley to be propelled by gravity and traverse to the bottom of the inclined cable. Like life, ziplining can be humbling. The older we get and the more of the world we've seen, the more we start to develop a routine. As we race across the cables, we see scenic views that may become a pattern. The days start to blend, the nights become mingled, and time passes us by.

Time is an abstract concept based on human perception. We should be constantly learning, reading about new subjects, trying new skills, practicing new languages. This is the best way to experience new things. That novelty should help you get more out of time, thus curbing the feeling that it's passing you by. Just like a zipline, life will pass by. If you blink, you'll miss the greatest journey afforded to you by your one and only Lord.

If you knew you only had a few years of life left, would you sit around and wait for death? I hope that you will summon all your courage and sense of adventure and attempt to finish your bucket list. I hope that you'll spend every possible second you can by living, laughing, and loving your favorite people and pets.

Ziplining through the majestic Grand Canyon brought admiration and astonishment to my soul. I was amazed at the towering cliffs carved by the copper-colored Colorado River. Perched at the edge of a desert view, I was astonished by its natural beauty and the immense canyons perfectly incised. I felt the rush of air as I was suspended by cables held by pulleys and propelled by gravity. It was like flying. For once in my life, I was like an eagle soaring through the sky with untamed wings and my eyes sparkling at the altitude of freedom.

I encourage you to be the best version of yourself. Because someday, when you're looking back on your life and your experiences, I don't want you to be full of regret and unhappiness. I want you to be proud of yourself and everything you've done. Soar to the clouds and float to the top of your dreams.

8. RANGE MASTER

"With the release of the trigger, my adrenaline blasted out."
SOSHINIE A. SINGH

Going to the shooting range to fire a gun at a target can be the same as one's life journey. I've been to many shooting ranges throughout my adult life, and each time I was able to experience firing different types of firearms. Each with a different handle, a distinct caliber size bullet, and dissimilar paper targets. You fire when you are ready with safety always in mind. Letting go of fear and regret, the actual process of shooting and releasing that trigger can be stress relieving.

Have you ever been really excited about a new opportunity but weren't able to pull the trigger and go for it? Was it because of fear, worry, or maybe over-analysis? And then, before you realized it, the opportunity had come and gone, and you missed out. Maybe you were nervous. Your hands started shaking and you couldn't keep your focus. You wanted to get the perfect shot, but your hands were bouncing all over the place. Your goal was practically within touching distance, and you didn't even get a shot off.

That wasn't the last time I experienced a similar event. There have been many times in my life where a potentially great opportunity came up and I never took the leap. I tend to think too much about everything and end up doing nothing. Maybe it is just plain fear of the unknown. Fear that I may lose what I already have if I reach out for something that might be better. Remember that risk is always better than regret.

Whatever the reason, I'm tired of it. I'm tired of always

playing it safe. Tired of missing out on the daring adventures in life because of worry, self-doubt, or over-scrutinizing. I was not put on this earth to travel only on the sheltered, flat roads. I want to live my life with moments of risk instead of always playing it safe and being guarded. I want to take the ups with the downs and, in the end, look back and be proud of myself for trying. I want to look back on my failures and laugh when I realize they were all worth it because I learned something about myself. Now I want to motivate you to pull that trigger and make magic happen.

9. MOUNTAIN BIKING

"It is the unknown around the corner that turns my wheels."

HEINZ STUCKE

Mountain biking can change your life. It is an amazing physical and mental challenge that encourages you to push your limits, try new things, meet new people, and explore wild destinations. You will learn to laugh at yourself, step out of your comfort zone, be proud of your accomplishments, and live in the moment, both on and off the trail.

Life is too short to sweat the small stuff. If it starts raining, you keep riding. If there is a tree down across the trail, you carry your bike over it. If you have a flat tire, you fix it and keep pedaling. You solve problems before you start worrying about them, a great skill to carry into your daily life. You might keep biking around the next corner, just to see what's there, because you never know.

There could be a majestic tree, a bird on the trail, or a scenic view to savor. Your curiosity feeds your passion, and it's in this position where you learn new things about yourself and your surroundings.

We will fall sometimes while bike riding. Every bump and bruise will have a story to tell, and you're ready to share. Your scars and soft spots are bright reminders of past adventures where you challenged yourself and came out on top. They are proof that you tested your limits, tried something new, and stepped out of your comfort zone.

My experience in mountain biking has brought me through scenic views and dead ends. I've overcome turbulent weather and crossed paths with mother nature's beautiful animals. Many times, I thought about turning back. I questioned my decisions. But there were also instances where I was glad that I was present in the moment. But like life, we must keep pedaling forward and have full confidence in our abilities. We should not be fearful because you never know what you will end up seeing. You never know what life will hand you in your pursuit of adventure.

Remember that when you're on the trail, you're in the moment. Recognize the benefits of transferring this mindset into your daily life with your work, relationships, and schooling. You will learn to commit all your attention to the task at hand and on the ride.

10. HALF DOME

"It's the hike you can't die without doing, and the hike you'll most likely die while doing."

UNKNOWN

Yosemite's Half Dome is perfectly inaccessible, being probably the only one of all the prominent points in Yosemite that has rarely been trodden by human foot. Its presence can be recognized from just about anywhere near the valley.

Considered one of the world's most difficult hikes, the Half Dome is a mighty giant I've always wanted to conquer. During my hike, while on the demanding and challenging trail, the brooding hulk of Half Dome high above kept my attention throughout. An early morning start took me up the dark trail. I was only able to listen to the beautiful sounds of the waterfalls and feel the cold soothing mist of the water rushing down from hundreds of feet above. My flashlight was the only light I utilized to lead me through until sunrise welcomed the seductress skies.

I knew I was in for a ride when I agreed to this hike. I never expected the feeling of accomplishment and affirmation that I can truly accomplish what I set my mind to. The next time I feel overwhelmed or daunted at a task, I'll remember that I conquered Half Dome and I'll get it done. At the crux of Half Dome, at the very top, is a smooth wall of rock that is a nearly vertical granite slab with tiny ripples for your hands and feet. It requires trusting the rubber friction beneath your shoes to stick to these ripples. I eventually made it to the top by utilizing my sheer willpower and overcoming the fatigue that set in. The view of Yosemite Valley was spectacular. I sat there for a moment to grasp and internalize the moment. Soon after, I began my long trek back to the starting point. It was a risky hike, but all journeys in life come with risks.

Keep your dreams alive. Understand that to achieve anything requires faith and belief in yourself, vision, hard work, determination, and dedication. Remember, all things are possible for those who believe. With preparation and a strong will, you too can accomplish any goal you set. Work hard for what you want; it won't come to you without a fight. You must be strong and courageous and know that you can do anything you put your mind to. If somebody puts you down or criticizes you, just keep believing in yourself and turn it into something positive.

The Half Dome hike and climb encompasses everything that a hike should be: a great challenge, beautiful scenery, fantastic camaraderie, and a feeling of accomplishment when it's over that will last a lifetime. I overcame Half Dome, standing at 8,839 feet after a hike of seventeen miles. This monster took ten hours to get to the summit and back. You, too, can overcome the hikes of your dreams and the challenges of tomorrow. Don't wait until it's too late.

11. WATER RAFTING

"May your choices reflect your hopes, not your fears."

NELSON MANDELA

When I went rafting on the beautiful Sacramento River, I couldn't have imagined how serene and peaceful the experience would be. But just like life, the calm waters were also intertwined with troubled and vigorous reservoirs. On that beautiful sunny day, I was able to feel the sun's ray of hope and the water's drenched pledge.

There's no other recreational sport quite as exciting, yet humbling, as water rafting. It's an activity that takes the non-adventurous person completely out of their comfort zone from the moment they step onto the raft until the moment the raft is pulled safely back to the shore. When we pay attention, we can glean great lessons through every experience, and water rafting is no exception. This rigorous sport can provide some of the greatest lessons in life you may not learn otherwise.

If you fall off the raft and into the water, you are no longer in control of your situation. You can only keep your head above water and breathe. The best way to paddle a river—and to live life—is to go with the flow. If you try to swim upstream against the current, you must put forth more effort than you would normally to make any progress. Going with the flow gives you momentum and keeps you propelling forward.

Just as a river is full of large rocks that appear to come from nowhere and snag your boat, life too has obstacles that show up when you're not expecting them. Understanding that there will always be obstacles to navigate will keep you flexible, adaptable, and ready when the unexpected happens. Take in the scenery along the way. Enjoy the twists and turns that life has to offer and spend it with the people you care about most. Have fun and enjoy the ride as you navigate through the river of life.

12. THE PRICE

*"I succeed because I am willing to
do the things you are not."*

TONY EVANS

We all face obstacles in our lives. Some of them are much bigger than others, but they are all barriers. The truth is that we can overcome any hurdle; we just need to know how. We need to focus on our abilities instead of the obstacle, on our capabilities instead of what is holding us back.

You are capable of more than you think, and you can overcome anything. Remind yourself of your value. You must be willing to do what others refuse to. You must conquer impediments that others find too difficult to attempt. What appears to be a hurdle is often an opportunity to move to a higher level in your personal or professional life. Keep your eyes, mind, and heart open to that possibility. If it weren't for the challenges you're facing now, you might not work to strengthen your talents and become more than you are today. You're wonderful the way you are, but there's always room to improve and opportunities for enhancement in the efficiency of your processes.

No matter what your barriers are, you must do something about them. They won't go away on their own. You can't avoid them forever. You can't run from them. You need a plan to overcome them. If you aren't sure what to do, you can start by creating a vision of what you want to accomplish. Your goal should be something you want more than anyone else. If you break your goal into smaller steps, you can create a plan to overcome your challenges. By following your plan, you will overcome the complication.

Some people take longer and even fail in their attempts to find success. But if you stay committed to moving forward, you can conquer any obstacle in your path. No matter how large your problem may be, you will need to fight against the odds. You are not shackled by fear, insecurity, or doubt. You are motivated by accomplishment, not pride. Pride consumes the weak and kills their hearts from within. If you fall, get up. If you are beaten, return. You will never stop getting better. You will never give up. That is why you will succeed.

13. DOGSLEDDING

"Life is like a dogsled team. If you ain't the lead dog, the scenery never changes."

LEWIS GRIZZARD

I was fortunate enough to ride with a pack of Siberian huskies through the cold and frigid landscape of northern Utah. I would not trade that experience for anything. Not only did I gain respect for the beloved dogs who train to go up and down these difficult paths deep in the snow, but I also learned a great deal about life in the cold of winter.

Dog sledding allows you to explore untouched backcountry terrain that would otherwise be inaccessible. Snowmobiles are not allowed, the terrain is too difficult, the snow is too deep, and the distance is too far to walk. I had to hold the dogs back while the musher hooked the entire team up or else they'd take off down the trail without me. The closer they got to take off, the more excited and louder their barks got. Like life, we must have patience and wait for our moment.

I knew I was in for an amazing day on the trail. I fed off the dogs' energy and became excited myself. Life can bring us adventures that we will remember for the rest of our lives. We must live in the moment before it's all over.

As the barks continued, I had to quickly get on the sled because the dogs were champing at the bit. We must be aggressive, but life also expects us to be submissive. Having a balance will keep us happy and help reduce mistakes. They were pulling on the sled so hard that I had to hold on to the brakes and keep the snow hook firmly in the ground or I'd be dragged behind. Once I let go of the brake, they instantly went quiet and started running.

In life, you may be eager to start a task, an ambition, or a goal. Helping others and showing support should always be on your agenda. You must find different ways to solve problems and keep tasks fun and challenging. Be a leader. Lead with passion. Show the way to others. Be a role model. Always take a deep breath and enjoy the beauty of life with your furry four-legged friends by your side.

14. MOUNT WHITNEY

"The mountains are calling, and I must go."

JOHN MUIR

Mount Whitney is the tallest peak in the continental and contiguous United States, and the trail to the summit offers a spectacular ascent through Sierra Nevada grandeur. Majestic granite cathedrals rise to the sky as you traverse through scenery alternating between fern-strewn pathways and monstrous boulders scattered like marbles shot by God's fingers.

After winning a prestigious permit allowing me to hike Mt. Whitney, I started my trek from the bottom of the Whitney Portal trail in the early morning. Making sure I had enough water and food to last the entire trip, I trekked to the top. The early morning darkness was overcome by a beautiful sunrise as I made my way up on the trail leading to the switchbacks. I eventually reached the crest and the unforgiving summit at 14,505 feet as scenic views passed me and jaw dropping sights caught my attention.

I felt a magnetic pull from the mountain. Verticality is commonplace, but the mountain's allure captivates the mind of the ones who want to study and preserve nature in its natural landscape. Hiking such phenomenal and demanding peaks pushes your stamina to the limit and requires months of preparation, hard work, and testing your physical abilities to the extreme. There is an inner need in all of us to climb a mountain. This helps us escape the real world and get lost in God's creation, to connect with a sacred moment. However, we can't stay in the moment forever. We have work to do, people to meet, and stories to share. When the mountains call, make sure you answer. The peak is waiting for you.

15. ROCK CLIMBING

"Rock climbing, perhaps life's most primitive and gratifying sport."

ERIC STEVENS

In life, as in rock climbing, there's no straight path to success. When a climber looks up at that rock wall, they may think they've figured out how to get to the top. But the truth is, no matter how experienced you are, halfway through the climb, you'll realize you need to take another route to reach the summit.

My first attempt at rock climbing was fueled by sheer adrenaline. Looking up at the mighty rock face, I wondered how I would have the energy to pull myself up using my arms and legs through the many rock faces. What would happen if I slipped, got tired, or if the fear of heights set in? The thoughts ran through my mind, but I had the willpower to deflect them. I knew I would get to the top no matter what. My fingers did get tired, and my hands developed blisters, but the fight to the top of that rock was worth it and the view was even better.

In life, we may think we have a clear plan to achieve what we have defined as success. What we tend to ignore is that our plans may change. There is no shame in taking a few steps back if it means making progress in the long run. We can climb any rock and successfully reach the top. We may not yet know exactly how to get there, but we can reach the top as long as we know what the top of the rock means to us.

Sometimes we not only take a step back, but we fall completely. All successful people do. That's how you learn and grow. What matters is that you get back up and continue climbing. You are more likely to accomplish this when you have people in your life who will tighten that rope when you need them to; people who will energize you and convince you to climb again.

Climbing challenges us to the core. It narrows our focus, has a competitive element and thrill factor, and it involves real teamwork. Answers come from having the courage to fail and being willing to climb tough obstacles. In life, you take hits. It isn't all offense. If we can learn to fall and find the resolve to keep climbing, we can learn a lot about ourselves and what it is to be human.

16. CAMPING

"Deep silence fell about the little camp, planted there so audaciously in the jaws of the wilderness."

ALGERNON BLACKWOOD

We have somehow forgotten to wake up to the sounds of birds singing or smell the fragrance of freshly bloomed flowers. We should all experience the forest, inhale the fresh air, and enjoy the beauty of the outdoors. The trees are calling; the rivers are roaring; the mountains are shouting, and the fire is bellowing.

Camping is an outdoor activity that involves overnight stays away from home. Leaving developed areas to spend time outdoors in more natural settings can provide great enjoyment. It teaches us self-reliance and teamwork. Camping can be enjoyed in conjunction with hiking and other outdoor activities. It is the only time where we can reflect on the elective nature and pursuit of our spiritual rejuvenation.

Camping not only lets you enjoy a vacation, but it also gives you ample space and time to think about yourself. The slow spaced life during camping is far from boring. Rather, it lets you discover yourself. It makes you realize who you really are. It might even help you find your true passion for life. Camping lets you shrug off your stresses, lift your mood, and boost your confidence to face challenges. It lets you realize there are many more important things in life beyond materialistic demands. Out in nature, you won't have the same luxuries you have at home.

I've been very fortunate to experience camping in many locations and settings. Each one provided a unique challenge that helped me learn about various survival techniques that can be used to sustain life in a natural environment. Apart from the necessities for human life, which include food, water, and shelter, I learned to use different tools for different means. I learned to deal with the possibility of having no medical aid. My favorite part was starting and tending to a fire. There were disappointments and successes, but through it all, I understood my physical and emotional limits. So, what you are waiting for? Disconnect from the artificial world and enjoy a memorable trip in the natural world, God's best gift to humankind.

17. PHOTOGRAPHY

*"We take photos as a return ticket to
a moment otherwise gone."*

ELLIOTT ERWITT

A person who takes photographs is a storyteller with an eye and experiences uniquely their own. They take photos to recall those experiences that have shaped and made them. They take photos to bridge distance and shorten time, to create a legacy for those who come after. One day, they take photos to feel like an artist; another day to identify as storytellers. They are musicians through their imaginative mind one night and a poet the next.

Have you ever felt there was something you always wanted to say but never had the courage to say it? Photography teaches you how to say something visually, and then the words follow through color. Taking a photo is like freezing time. It's about finding something interesting in an ordinary place. Everything you see is stored in your soul and how you see things becomes the reason for your existence. We project who we are to the world and observe the beauty that surrounds us in our own unique way. Photographs bring life to writing and writing can bring life to your vision to find those perfect moments to capture. Photography is an art and, just like writing, you can use your imagination to bring life to the world's bleakest stages.

We tend to gravitate toward our cameras when we come across places and things that give us meaning. Nothing is more interesting than reality, so remember to photograph the world as it is. Take photos, capture images and, when all the portraits are done, put the camera down. Let the last photo you didn't capture live on in the quiet place of your memory and revisit it often.

18. THE INTELLECT

"It seems that the more places I see and experience, the bigger I realize the world to be. The more I become aware of, the more I realize how relatively little I know of it, how many places I have still to go, how much more there is to learn."

ANTHONY BOURDAIN

I've been blessed to observe many sites. I've been honored to experience many scenes. The more locations I visit, the vaster the world becomes. I begin to understand how insignificant my knowledge is and my ability to grasp the universe. I am enlightened to know that the mind never rests. Intellect will never obtain clarity. Wisdom tells us we have far to go and the place we seek will never be reached.

When we are looking for an enriching and transformative journey, we gravitate toward learning new skills, dealing with the unexpected, and engaging in activities to improve mental wellbeing. An adventurous life can bring you new experiences and environments that can stimulate creativity and inspire innovative thinking. What kind of adventures are you interested in exploring for your personal growth?

I hope you see all the places your heart desires. I hope you love the things you've always wanted to hold on to. I hope you gain the wisdom to understand your capabilities and your imperfections. And I hope the Lord directs you to the path of righteousness where your mind can be free to fly to the places you only dreamed of. Your success awaits you, one adventure at a time. May peace be upon your journey to nobility.

19. BASKETBALL

"Be the best version of yourself in anything that you do. You don't have to live anybody else's story."

STEPHEN CURRY

Life can be unpredictable. No matter how hard you try to grasp it, it will always have its way with you. Each bounce, every step you take, leads to another aspect of the game of life. Like dribbling a basketball, it has its ups and downs. You win some and you lose some. Sometimes you make the shot, other times you miss.

It's important to understand that you can't accomplish great things by yourself. You will need support, a team, a group of individuals to tackle the greatest problems and obstacles with you. Self-actualization is a deeply personal yet universal goal. While it's ultimately an individual journey that starts within, a strong supportive network can amplify your progress.

Just like basketball, you shoot hoops to be successful; you defend when you meet an opponent. You pass the ball to have someone support you or reach out for a helping hand. Those supportive people are often family members, but also your friends for life. You dribble to keep up and to make it to success while making sure you follow the rules of the game. You avoid violations that are like breaking the law in life.

In basketball, you cannot succeed unless you believe in yourself and your teammates. It is this belief that gives you confidence. You must have confidence that you will make that crucial shot to win the game. Similarly in life, you must have self-assurance. You must have faith in your abilities. Without this, you cannot be successful or happy.

Too often, people don't follow their desires and goals but try to fulfill a particular life scenario. Don't allow the noise of other people's opinion and drown out your inner voice. Have the courage to follow your heart and intuition and dribble past your fears. Shoot for the stars and assist others on your way to success.

20. THE MOUNTAIN

> *"Mountains know secrets we need to learn. That it might take time, it might be hard, but if you just hold on long enough, you will find a strength to rise up."*

TYLER KNOTT GREGSON

What is it about mountains that encapsulate our greatest adventures and triumph? Is it their unpredictable force and unmerciful weather? Their towering, grandiose height? Their demanding presence? I've always wanted to summit the highest mountains and climb the highest peaks. Every hiking list of mine includes some type of mountainous terrain. Knowing the difficulty of the trek depends on the altitude of the mountain.

Humans have always been fascinated with mountains—admiring their beauty from afar and from their summits, attempting to reach the top of even the tallest and most treacherous mountains. Even our legendary heroes lived among mountains. We are fascinated with stories and quotes about mountains, the challenges we face climbing them, their role in nature, and of course their symbolism to life: our journey, struggles, and triumphs. Hold your vision of where you want to go, what you want to do, and who you want to be in your heart. Take the step to the summit of your ambitions and all that your soul aims for.

I want to inspire you to appreciate the journey, overcome your obstacles, and summit mountains, both literally and metaphorically. It can be difficult, but there is no pleasure in life if your goal is always attainable. Building the strength to accomplish your goals and perhaps you'll start to decode your own mysteries. Get outside and adventure on!

21. CHOICES

"The world meets nobody halfway."

SYLVESTER STALLONE

In life, there are winners and there are quitters. We don't always get what we want, but maybe that's because we believe we can't get what we desire. The world we live in is not a place for the softhearted. It may be cruel and at times unfair. Often, we only call for trouble when our true intentions are otherwise.

Some of us think life is tough. But we only have one life, and we must make something great of it. Until we realize that, we won't be able to know our true potential. There are no shortcuts. There are no miracles. Either you want it, or you will settle for something less. Life demands effort and persistence. If you're not willing to meet the world head-on, you may miss out on what you're looking to achieve.

You will eventually face situations where you want to be quiet. You will face tough decisions. You will be tested. You will face obstacles that will seem unavoidable. In some ways, though, it will help. It will keep you going by transferring energy into you. You will feel like it is telling you not to stop, to keep seeking what you were supposed to find; And you will know you have to keep going. There is no time to stop in life.

If you want something, you must go get it yourself. Whether it's a career, a goal, or a pursuit of greatness, you must do what it takes to earn it. It won't meet you halfway. If you want to be with the love of your life, you must give your full effort. If you leave it up to someone else for your own happiness or fulfillment, you will ultimately be disappointed. Take responsibility for your own decisions and actions. Be willing to get ahead in life by choosing to do the things that most of society is not willing to do.

22. DEATH VALLEY

"We live in a rainbow of chaos."

PAUL CEZANNE

Living in a rainbow of chaos is a metaphorical expression that suggests living in a state of capricious, ever-changing circumstances with moments of beauty and wonder. Chaos implies disorder, confusion, and unpredictability, while a rainbow is often associated with beauty, diversity, and hope. Together, they create an image of a life that is full of ups and downs, where unexpected events are constantly shaping and reshaping one's experiences.

Living in a variegation of disorder could be interpreted as living in a world that is both exciting and challenging. One where we must navigate through unpredictable situations and emotions while also recognizing the beauty and joy that can arise from those experiences. It may require embracing the unpredictability of life, finding ways to adapt to changing circumstances, and learning to appreciate the beauty that can emerge from even the most challenging situations.

Like the rainbow-colored mountains of the Artists Palette, develop your success through the chaotic experience of your life's painting—the colors representing your moods, the textures indicating your accomplishments, the shadows representing your setbacks, and unpainted areas representing the potential awaiting you.

My visit to Artists Palette in Death Valley National Park, with its technicolor, kaleidoscopic display of multicolored rock, was a must see to be believed trip. Located near the hub of Furnace Creek, on the west facing side of the Black Mountains, it is one of the most photographed spots in Death Valley. Tucked behind an unassuming yellow landscape, the rainbow of Artists Palette is the highlight with a stunning glimpse into the desert's colorful volcanic past. This hidden gem with painted hills is truly a majestic site to behold, an inspiration to add all the colors of life to your next adventure.

23. THE LIGHT

"There is always enough light for the one who wishes to see."

IMAM ALI

Our dreams are the lifeblood of our existence. Our reverie and aspirations fuel us with purpose, focus, and a deeper meaning, inspiring us to share our gifts with the world. What we desire to create warms our heart, fires up our resolve, and clarifies our mind through an esteemed vision we caress within.

Everything begins as a seed, a bud that we nurture to full blossom. Through the mosaic of our minds, we are given divine flashes of insight and sparks of poetic beauty that we get to mold and shape. Our dreams reflect who we are in our bravest and most courageous moments. Learn to open your mind and see. Learn to observe through obscurity when you have a contrary disposition.

The journey to our dreams and grand ambitions is often fraught with failure, hardship, and inner discord as we strive to make something real out of what begins as a lucid impression in our minds and a yearning in our hearts. This is where the true test of our inner grit and resilience begins to unfold, where we can choose to go all the way or not at all.

Our dreams demand wholehearted and emphatic effort, testing us all the way, yet whispering through the quiet recesses of our innermost being to just go the distance. If you truly want to succeed, you'll always find a way to do it, no matter how difficult it may be. You will be questioned. You will be doubted. Your vision will be obscured. But for the one who wishes to win, there will always be enough light in the darkness to forge your way to success.

24. DECISIONS

*"It's the scary choices that end up
being the most worthwhile."*

MELISSA JOY KONG

As adults, the decisions we make can be complicated. We've got to decide which jobs to take, which relationships to pursue, which city to move to, how to take care of our money and sometimes even which trail to hike. As teenagers, we must decide what college to attend, what career path to follow, and how to handle setbacks. It's exhausting. If you are on the cusp of making one of these monstrously scary decisions, know that you are not alone. While it's never easy, there are ways to ensure that you make the choice that is right for you.

While our choices certainly matter, we can easily put way too much emphasis on them. After all, the things in life that really dictate the course of our future are often random, unplanned occurrences. Sometimes the decisions we make really are life changing, and sometimes they aren't.

Often, when we feel stuck in a decision, it's because we have a profound sense of anxiety associated with it. While anxiety can carry a sense of immediacy and randomness, it always comes from a deeper source below the surface. Give yourself time to reflect on what the source of that anxiety is. What about this decision scares you? Are you afraid of other people's advice? The people in your life who know you, love you, and want good things for you should be your lifeline. Meet with them and ask for their honest assessment of your situation. Seek out people who will be open and honest with you.

It's time to put your imagination to work. Take every side of the decision you must make and visualize its future. But more importantly, think about the worst possible outcome. Think about what your life will look like if this decision fails. While this sounds like a grim mind game, you might find that the worst possible outcome isn't as bad as you feared. If you can live with it, then that's something to consider. You will reach a point in life where you know it's time to take a leap. Make a choice, commit to it, and don't look back. You have no ability to know what the future will hold, so take that step into the unknown and enjoy life.

25. CONQUER

*"Life can be a big hulking toward above
you and you must conquer it."*

UNKNOWN

Exceedingly or increasingly violent, life rises to an extreme height or intense degree to which you may feel helpless. Like a towering rage, life will humble you. This is how I felt when I first encountered the mighty Golden Gate Bridge in San Francisco. Its magnificent span is anchored by two towers that reach 746 feet skyward. This iconic landmark stood tall above my presence and reminded me of how insignificant we are, and that was very humbling.

At some point, life will humble you. You'll see love come and go. Accomplishments will turn to failures. Smiles will disappear with the new storm. Abandon all selfishness and pride in your human power and stand humbled, meek, and submissive as a servant to your Lord above all else. Remove arrogance and pride, for you will see that we are nothing in this vast universe.

But it is a great irony of the human soul that when we become humbler and more submissive to the Creator of the World, we fall into a grave trap. We tend to grow arrogant because we feel our level of submission is better than that of others. Don't ever compare yourself to others. You are unique. If you are humble, nothing can touch you, neither praise nor disgrace, because you know what you are.

And so, I continued walking on the bridge, watching as the towers stared at my every step, reminding me of life's goals and the ability to conquer whatever my heart desired, no matter how big or small. Remember that your greatest obstacle can present you with the most opportunity. Don't allow the size of your troubles to discourage your success. Your willingness to pursue something you do not yet have will be your motivation to overcome any goal.

26. BRAVERY

"Love asks us that we be a little braver than is comfortable, a little more generous, a little more flexible."

NORMAN MAILER

In order to understand bravery, one must understand fear. Fear is a cruel enemy. Most people don't like to get to know their enemies. Truth is, one must not only know their enemies, but it is infinitely beneficial to understand them as well. Most people have a fear of rejection and failure. These are the two contemporary greatest human fears alongside death, a long-standing human fear. But some also fear being misunderstood, in an existential kind of way.

The most profound thing about fear is that there is no escaping it. Fear is an enemy you will battle until death, but knowing it is inescapable is exactly why bravery is of the utmost necessity in life. Fear paralyzes, while bravery frees. Fear chooses mediocre, while bravery takes the risk of chance, a chance that could bring greatness or defeat. Fear always leads to regret, while bravery leads to knowledge.

Bravery requires endurance because it requires persistence and perseverance. It keeps you going when all odds are against you. Sometimes bravery means having the prudence to pause, to sit in silence, and to be okay. It means putting up the fight of your life and fighting until the very end. Sometimes bravery means searching for the things and the people who make you feel alive; to take risks, to be a long shot and an outlier. It means to be grateful and content and satisfied with your present state.

But bravery must also be an act of love. Whether of a thing or person or place, bravery must be manifested through love. And to be brave, you must accept that the great love of anything may result in heartbreak, pain, and disappointment. To be brave, you must be willing to risk the possibility of a terrifying ending. To be brave is to be alive and to live in such a way that the world knows you are afraid, but you love more than you fear, and your success is the ultimate outcome.

27. THE STAGE

"Life doesn't always have a Hollywood ending."

DARK NIGHT BEACON

Your life isn't meant to follow a Hollywood storyline. There are happy endings and there are sad ones. There are tragedies and unresolved endings. Some endings will make you cry and others will bring you joy. There will be heartbreaks along the way and beautiful endings. Sometimes love will be a part of your life. Falling in love takes time and work. It isn't always rainbows and butterflies. If things were perfect and good all the time, we wouldn't realize they were. We need the downs to make us realize what the ups feel like.

It's painful to realize a relationship with someone you love and care for may come to an end. Heartbreaks happen, but we learn from them, and we learn so much about ourselves afterward. We also experience pain. Pain is temporary and sometimes necessary to push us into the next phase of our life. Love comes in all different shapes and sizes and finds you at various points in your life. Each side of love will have a different edge and may not fit with the puzzle of your life. You don't always discover this misshaped edge immediately. Oftentimes it takes months or even years to realize the piece may not belong.

Not everyone we meet is meant to be in our lives forever. God has a plan for everyone, along with lessons that are meant to be learned. Heartbreak hurts, but it is painfully recoverable. There are different types of love in this world, and some aren't meant to be lifelong.

When we stop comparing our real lives to a Hollywood love story, we stop creating fantasy scenarios in our heads. These scenarios are not real, and when we expect them to be, we set ourselves up for failure. Don't settle for false happy endings. You can't love someone until you love yourself. This sounds cliché, but you will believe its truth once you really do love yourself and are in a relationship. So next time you pull out a Hollywood movie, don't look at it as a roadmap for your life. When you look at your life for what it is and discover what true happiness feels like, it often fills the void better than a Hollywood happily ever after.

28. THE STORM

"Even the strongest blizzards start with a single snowflake."

SARA RAASCH

My first tromp in the snow was a little risky, but my mutual love for hiking and the outdoors is unmatched. I was confident that I would reach my destination, even on the coldest of days on the slopes. My first experience in snowshoeing reminded me of the importance of being self-aware and knowing my surroundings. A physically demanding trek on uneven terrain required effort to lift my feet with each step. Winter weather conditions can be challenging, and it comes with risks. In life, it's important to be ready for any challenge that surrounds you, even when things initially may appear calm. Getting lost can become reality when the trail often lacks marked or packed-in trails. Life will not always give you a smooth trail to walk upon.

Snowshoeing is a killer winter workout. Uphill at sea level is one thing, but at altitude, it's another beast to conquer. Snowshoeing allows you to roam freely without restrictions. Once you invest in a pair of snowshoes, there's little to no additional costs. I am blessed to have had the opportunity to trek atop Oregon's Crater Lake and experience the winter wonderland through the preserved volcanic environment. The adventure inspired awe from the cliffs of the Cascade Mountain Range. Many hiking trails become snowshoeing terrain come wintertime at this pristine and unforgettable national park. No tune ups, lessons, lift tickets, or crowds to deal with.

Imagine being surrounded by nothing but untouched

snow and utter silence, except for the crunch of snow beneath your feet. Most importantly, panoramic and breathtaking scenery awaits. That's the back-country experience so many skiers seek during these cold winter months, and now I understand why. I also learned it's not uncommon for skiers and snowshoers to share the same wintery terrain.

Unlike some winter sports that take up an entire day and aren't always conducive to doing in groups, snowshoeing is a fun and a social activity that almost everyone can enjoy. Seasoned hikers can head for hillier trails, but you can also get a great workout on the flat trails, too. All you must do to up the intensity is step off the snowpack and do a few minutes in knee-deep powder. Like a hike or a run, you can go for as little or as long as you like. Just hit the trail and enjoy the beauty that surrounds you. Snowshoeing has rekindled my love for winter and snow, and even for being outdoors in frigid temperatures. When the storm arrives, take a trek in the snow and venture off trail. Start the biggest uproar and take charge of your success.

29. HORSEBACK RIDING

"There are many wonderful places in the world, but one of my favorite places is on the back of my horse."

ROLF KOPFLE

I have been fortunate to have the opportunity to ride a horse on multiple occasions. Horses have taught me many life lessons. Things like responsibility, commitment, critical thinking, and positive communication. They have taught me that perseverance is key if I want to get anywhere in life.

There are horses who have made me work harder to get a lead change or counter canter. They gave me the determination and perseverance to get it done and prove my riding ability. Horses have taught me that I need to apply patience to my entire life, not just one specific thing. There will always be a horse to teach me to wait with my body and wait for the perfect distance, otherwise they will chip.

But most importantly, horses have taught me that it is okay to fail and that it is okay to change my path. They have taught me that I don't have to win to be great. I need to work hard and have a positive attitude. I need to fix my mistakes and learn from them if I want to get better. I don't have to win a ribbon to know I had a good ride.

I am forever grateful to all the other horses I surrounded myself with in the past. Yes, these animals have taught me, but they also saved me. Most importantly, they showed me a life worth living. I don't need all the money in the world; I don't need anything fancy in my life. If I am happy and riding a horse, life becomes meaningful. I am forever blessed by these four-legged creatures, and no matter where I go in life, I know that if I have a horse, I will be just fine.

The next time you ride a horse, remember that developing a relationship with the horse requires trust and respect. Like life, you must trust the process while also maintaining control over your choices and actions. As you ride, you must move in sync with the horse, just like you must harmonize your goals and circumstances to keep progressing in life.

30. THE TREASURE

"The cave you fear to enter holds the treasure you seek."
JOSEPH CAMPBELL

Fear lies. Don't let it hinder you from living life to the fullest, because the greatest thing in life is truly to be found behind the curtain of fear. When you get to the other side of it, you'll be amazed. That's where life is, but most people live within the bounds of their fear. They believe the lies fear tells them, so they are too scared to venture out and take risks.

If you take a step outside your comfort zone, the Universe will meet you and help you take the next, and the next after that. The cosmos responds to your actions and meets you where you are to lift you up to the next level of your life if you just let it. But the first step is yours to take, and that is the most difficult one, especially if you believe more in your fear than in yourself and all the possibilities life has in store for you.

Often our first instinct when feeling fear is to pull back into our comfort zone or distract ourselves with something else so we can escape the uncomfortable feeling. No one is coming to rescue you. No one will make you find the entrance to that mysterious cave. No one will tell you how to navigate that dark abyss. No one will magically map your destination. There is no hero in the story of your life but you. It will ultimately be you who will have to walk into that dark cave alone.

We must confront what scares us most. The barriers we put up to protect ourselves from fear are also the barriers to unlocking our potential. There's also a metaphorical richness in how fear can be both a guardian and a gateway, guarding valuable insights or experiences we may not even know we need.

I can't promise that you'll get to the treasure at the end of your journey. If you're committed to being in that cave, taking continuous steps in the direction of your greatest potential, it's the journey that will transform you more than the treasure. It really is the path, not the destination. So, take a deep breath and start your journey. The cave is waiting for you to enter.

CHAPTER III

FAITH

Understanding your place in the universe is the most exhilarating feeling. It is accomplished through sincere gratitude and gratefulness of the existence around you. The deeper your grief and struggle, the closer your union will be with the Lord. If you're not a believer of God, I can assure you that in this chapter, you will realize the existence of a higher power. Your imagination can help pave your understanding of the supreme being that is responsible in our world and beyond. Your belief and trust in God will be tested, but hold steadfast, because the Lord has a plan for you. Consider yourself blessed because the Lord's grace resides in you.

1. THE TREE

> *"My strength is trust. I know nothing about my father. I know nothing about the thousands of children that every year spring out of me. I live out the secret of my seed to the very end and I care for nothing else. I trust that God is in me. I trust that my labor is holy. Out of this trust I live."*

HERMANN HESSE

Since the beginning of time, trees have captured humankind's imagination through their wonder, and we find ourselves astonished by them. We find inspiration in their strength, deeply rooted in the earth. Their trunks and branches are a wonder of nature because they stand sturdy and impenetrable most of the time, yet they can flex and sway with the wind when needed.

Trees abide by their own laws. Their roots branch out in their struggle to fulfill and represent themselves. To be a strong tree is to be holy, and nothing is more exemplary. Trees are like the human species. Each ring of a tree represents a year of life and growth. Just like when we are born with raw instincts that form our personality as we age, we develop new rings of emotions.

A new ring develops, and we no longer cry for everything. We cry because we're upset. We get happy, jealous, angry, disgusted, or scared, and sometimes all of these within the same day. The ring that made us cry will eventually be covered by the ring of intelligence, and you learn to contain your emotions when they aren't welcome. Later, intelligence is coated with some life experience or a traumatic situation that grants us the ability to understand both other people's behavior and our own to face the storms of life.

One day, you'll be stripped of some of these rings you developed over your lifetime. You'll be left with the vulnerable side of you. The side that doesn't know logic and reason, that has no clue what's happening or even a slight idea of how to heal yourself. We must stay strong through all the adversaries we face. Our trust in others will be questioned. Our faith in humanity will be altered. Our belief in the goodness of others will be shaken. Through it all, remain humble and allow God to guide you through the growth and journey.

Trees are sanctuaries. If we speak to them, we can learn the truth. By understanding that we have a purpose to fulfill in life, we fight and move forward, trusting that our patience will be rewarded. We place our life and faith in God to fulfill the duties of humankind by looking for things to be grateful for and being honest about our doubts to help us trust.

2. THE PURPOSE

"You play the hand you're dealt. What I am, I am of my own choice. I don't know if I'm happy, but I'm content."

UNKNOWN

Many of us are searching for our life's purpose. That's not something we can easily uncover; it unfolds over a lifetime. But what we should do is create meaning for our lives. We can take the hand we're dealt and make the most of what we're given. How can you be a better person? How can you contribute to yourself, to those close to you, and to the world? How can you find the courage to pursue what you're passionate about?

The fact that we weren't born rich or talented shouldn't matter. Some of us may not be able to write or draw. Others were never encouraged to do what they always wanted. It doesn't matter because we should stop comparing our life with others. Everyone comes into life with challenges. The catch is each person has different sets of challenges. While you might envy someone's ease at making friends, they might wonder how you land jobs so easily. While you might wish you had wealth, someone might crave the freedom and simplicity of your life. The grass may look greener, but every pasture comes with its own weeds.

We come into life with certain lessons to learn. Our life circumstances, including our strengths and limitations, are the optimal ones for learning those lessons. Some of those lessons will be exhilarating and some will be miserable. If we can embrace even the tough ones, we can minimize the pain and struggle of going through them. When we don't learn from our experiences, we're doomed to repeat them. By facing them squarely and doing whatever it takes, we can move on to grander experiences.

You are the person you are today because of your own choices. You had the courage to pursue the real meaning of your life. You made the most of your situation to contribute to your community, your family. You may not be dealt a fair hand, but have faith that you have a purpose in life. You may not be always happy, but you can be content.

3. GRATEFULNESS

*"Don't take things for granted because
they might not be there tomorrow."*

UNKNOWN

Very few people can see the impact of what they do now and how it relates to their future. Do you regret the present, where you have no idea what is happening and don't have the slightest conception of long-term consequences? Or do you have remorse for the past, where you can take your time to see things as they were? People make mistakes and leave the things they love the most. They fail to appreciate the good things they once had and, as a result, will continuously regret their decision.

People tend to always want something more, something new, but sometimes the most valuable things are what has always been with us. We won't always get what we desire, but that doesn't mean we will never obtain our aspirations. Happiness will never come to those who fail to appreciate what they already have. Just like you don't know what you have until it's gone, you don't know what you've been missing until it arrives.

Have faith because life is precious. Longevity is not granted to everyone. You'll never know what you are going to lose. Someone's last days will come way too soon, and there will be so much you want to do and say. Tomorrow is not guaranteed. Be grateful and remember to love with all your heart. The universe is sending us a message to live fully each day. The promise of tomorrow may not come true, but you can pledge to always remain humble and accept each day as a gift from God.

4. THE REVELATION

*"You may not understand today or tomorrow,
but eventually God will reveal why you
went through everything you did."*

UNKNOWN

Sometimes I question why I was chosen to endure that traumatic experience. Was it my fault I had my innocence taken away from me? Some questions in life may never be answered. Those who believe have the faith to understand that everything that happens is because God wills it. If I believe in the Lord, why didn't He prevent it? If God is All-Knowing and All-Powerful, why doesn't He want what's best for us? Horrific tragedies, pain, and suffering continue throughout the world. We face temptations, sorrow, and trials in our own lives. We might not always know why evil things happen, but it can help us to remember what we do know.

Choice and accountability for our actions are necessary for our spiritual growth. If God wants us to reach our divine potential, He will not force us to make the right decisions and He will not interfere with the consequences of those choices. Although God doesn't infringe on our choices, He does ease the burden of our afflictions and strengthen us to bear them.

Going through something difficult will allow you to empathize with that experience and with people who face a similar challenge. Have you seen others who experience sorrow from difficult circumstances and turn their pain into an empowering cause? Trials and tribulations can enable us to show others genuine compassion. It opens our eyes to those who are suffering and in turn makes us more empathetic, charitable, and influential human beings. Remember that one day we will look back at everything we had to overcome in gratitude because it helped us become who we were destined to be.

In life, we may not understand everything we endure. We may not comprehend the occurrences in our daily lives. We will question our faith and dwell on our future. But God is the best of planners. One day you will know why you went through what you did. You will understand the reason behind the pain, the suffering, the wait. It will be revealed when you least expect it.

The very thing you hate the most is what God wants to use for good in your life. This is called redemptive suffering. It is when you go through a problem or a pain for the benefit of others. There are many causes for the problems, pains, and suffering in your life. Sometimes difficulties present and struggles happen because we bring them upon ourselves. But in some of our problems, we're innocent. We've been hurt by the pain, stupidity, and sins of others. And some of the pain in our life is for redemptive suffering. God often allows us to go through a problem so that we can then help others. The next time you begin to ponder God's plan for your life, I encourage you to move forward and have faith. And when you seek His will earnestly, you will find it. Why? Because God is great.

5. DOUBT

*"Doubt is a pain too lonely to know
that faith is his twin brother."*

KHALIL GIBRAN

Doubt is mistrust and indecision and a horrible emotion to feel or absorb. Whether you doubt yourself, someone else, or a situation, it is a very lonely place to be. Why? Because you don't know what to do or say since you are doubting even yourself, and you are in a state of indecision. There is no strength behind doubt. There is no faith behind indecision. Without faith and strength, your chances of reconciling are few.

Our minds must use all the theories, philosophies, and teachings we've gained along the way to sort out the details and make a decision based on faith. Doubt is the opposite of faith and has no conclusion. We don't know which way to turn, what road to take, and faith must be strong in these times of despair. We must have faith that we will weigh the options and make the right decision for ourselves and others. Faith gives us strength, and when we feel strong, we can make choices that are in our best interest.

I believe faith is the credence that a Higher Power exists, created us, loves us, and is watching over us until we end our journeys here on earth and begin them with Him. To doubt the existence of God is to live either in fear or blindly believing we come from nothing and then die realizing our mistake. Doubt is a disease of the heart with respect to understanding truth and falsehood. In doubt, there is suspense, confusion, two-mindedness, and wandering. It deprives rightfulness of truth and the refutation of falsehood.

6. THE MOMENT

"There is a loneliness more precious than life.
There is a freedom more precious than the world.
Infinitely more precious than life and the world
is that moment when one is alone with God."

RUMI

There can be many types of relationships in this world: a bond between a couple, a parent to a child, an alliance with friends, siblings, coworkers, students, and family. But a relationship with God is above all. There is only one God, the Creator and Sustainer, and to Him we shall return.

Spending time alone with a loved one provides the opportunity to truly know that person. Spending time alone with God is no different. When we're alone with God, we draw closer to Him and get to know Him in a different way than we do in group settings. God desires alone time with us. He wants a personal relationship with us. He created us as individuals, knitting us in the womb. God knows the intimate details of our lives and He invites us to come to Him and know Him.

We all have a hunger to know why we're here. We possess an insatiable desire for love, passion, and purpose. Maybe you've had a relationship with God for years. Maybe you're still trying to figure out if God even exists or if He is knowable. Wherever you are on your journey with

God, know that God longs to satisfy your hunger. Spending time alone with Him rids our minds of distraction so that we can focus on Him and hear His Word. Abiding in Him, we enjoy the intimacy to which He calls us and come to truly know Him. We are taught responsibility, purpose, balance, discipline, and simplicity. The choice of how you will spend your time is entirely up to you.

I pray that you will be filled with the longing and strength to spend time with God. God is a limitless ocean of grace and help. All that's necessary to receive from Him is some time and an open heart. God calls you His beloved and longs for you to know Him to greater depths. May your day be marked by His transcendent peace and tangible nearness, and your nights by His holy grace and immense forgiveness.

7. POWER OF GOD

"You have to do the best with what God gave you."

FORREST GUMP

We must work heartily with our Lord always in mind, knowing that from the Lord we will receive the inheritance as our reward. We are serving the one and only God. Happiness is God's will for us, and He has provided the keys that will bring happiness, contentment, and joy regardless of our circumstances. It starts by learning to be happy with ourselves.

Could it be that you're unhappy with yourself because you're not perfect? Or maybe you are missing something in your life. Is there someone or something you yearn for and just can't seem to get a hold of? God doesn't require us to be perfect because He made us, and He knows we're human and will make mistakes. Your faith alone will allow you to be your best during difficult times. If giving your best is not enough, rely on your Lord to give you another chance to be better.

Our job is to get up every day and do the best we can. And when we fail, we must get right with God, receive His forgiveness, and move forward. We need to quit being so hard on ourselves and enjoy our lives right where we are. As believers, we are containers that God wants to fill with His goodness and light. Then we're to carry that goodness and light to a dark world, sharing it with people everywhere we go. Don't be afraid of your flaws; acknowledge them. Quit worrying about what you're not and give God what you are. Yes, people will leave you, and storms of misunderstanding will disrupt your friendships. But always have hope and patience. You can accomplish wonderful things. You can make somebody happy. You can encourage, edify, and exhort those around you. You can use your gifts and talents to serve God and do the best you can.

8. PRAYER

"If you want to see the sunshine, sometimes you just have to bow your head, say a prayer, and weather the storm."

FRANK LANE

You prayed for the answer, for guidance, for strength. You prayed for all of this and now you have your head bowed and you are wondering why. It's time to stop and think about what it is that you have asked for. There are so many reasons for the tough times that we go through in our life. I'm sure we have all experienced that feeling when we don't really have a clue *what* we are feeling. When so many amazing things are happening in our life while other parts are going up in smoke.

Just as you was starting to get life figured out, things came crashing down around you. But then you realized something spectacular, that maybe this is part of the journey to figuring your life out. You haven't fully accepted this yet. It is a scary reality to be facing, but this is an important part of the journey. Prayer is necessary for the soul to stay healthy and sustained. Spiritual nourishment and a connection to the Lord is necessary for protection, forgiveness, and to develop a sense of unity with your fellow human beings.

The problem is that we want everything to go our way, and we forget it is God's way that we should be trying to find. That is where we get lost. Things were starting to go our way, and we were getting too comfortable in our own plans. As a result, we weren't following God's plan.

It is hard to walk through the storms of our lives. It is hard to understand, and we often find ourselves questioning why we are being punished. But we forget that on the other side of those battles is a new day. We can start a new chapter, and God will be with us as we get through it. So, take a deep breath, close your eyes, and go to sleep. Wake up early and watch that beautiful sunrise and thank God for giving you another day. Then take that day and make it yours.

9. THE EYE

*"Everything that is made beautiful and fair and
lovely is made for the eye of the one who sees."*

RUMI

Before you finish reading this sentence, billions of operations will have been completed inside your eyes. However fantastic it may seem; you possess an example of the universe's ultimate technology. No one has ever come close to fully grasping it, let alone inventing anything remotely similar. Whatever you have in your life is meaningful because of your senses. Your family, your house, your job, your friends, and everything else in your surroundings you can quickly identify thanks to your vision.

Without eyes, you could never get a quick, complete sense of everything that's happening around you. Without them, you could never imagine colors, forms, scenes, human faces, or what the word beauty means. But you do have eyes, and thanks to them, you can now read this book before you.

To see an object, all you must do is to turn your gaze toward it. You don't need to bother giving "project, capture, analyze" orders to your eyes, the optical nerves running to the back of your brain, nor to the brain itself. Like many people, you may never have realized what a miracle it is that thousands of independent processes can operate in perfect harmony to enable you to see.

Those who best understand how irreplaceable this blessing is are people who lose their eyesight later in life. In the event that you are struck blind, your long list of lifetime plans and ambitions might be sidelined by one wish: to regain your lost eyesight. Without a doubt, no gift in the world is more valuable. You would experience no greater happiness than having the ability to see. And that is why I have a deep admiration for those who are visually impaired.

Be grateful. Trust your Creator. Your vision is a gift. At this very moment, if you are not acknowledging the unique blessing of your eyes to the Gracious One who has granted it to you, then you are being deeply ungrateful, a state of mind that is shared by a substantial part of humanity.

10. IMPERMANENT

"I'm so afraid because I'm so profoundly happy. Happiness like this is frightening. They only let you be this happy if they're preparing to take something from you."

KHALED HOSSEINI

Life will not always be full of happiness. You must also endure pain and suffering. Whenever you are happy, sadness is always a short distance away. Whenever you are sad, happiness is hiding around the next corner. As raw as it may sound, it is a simple but difficult truth to swallow, because moments can and will change at any time.

Some smiles hide deep secrets. Some eyes cry the most tears. Some hearts feel the most pain. It is in the taking away that our true love and trust are revealed, which is a great mercy to us and for others. Often, the most valuable, satisfying, beneficial, and longest lasting gifts we receive and pass along to others come through the experiences of our losses.

There will come a time when you are extremely happy, and everything is going your way. Happiness in this form is frightening because it will eventually be taken away from you in one form or another. It is inevitable. It will be a test of your patience and faith. It can be quite humbling.

You will suffer frustration. You will endure collapse and insufficiency. But know that whatever your misfortune may be, you'll get through it. Never regret a day in your life. Developing trust and confidence in the Lord strengthens your conviction and credence. Good days give you happiness and bad days give you experience. Both are essential in life because they are God's blessings. Understand that He has a purpose for you and one day you will come to understand His immense mercy and greatness.

11. THE MOMENT

"The two most important days of your life are the day you are born and the day you find out why."

MARK TWAIN

Until we are born, there isn't much to our lives, at least not as we know it. But at some point in our existence, we find out why we are here. The divine destiny is all that has happened and will happen, which will come to pass as written by God. Do you ever find yourself asking why you were brought to this world? What the reason is for your birth?

We all have unique talents which lend themselves to specific tasks. There are things that only you can do, people only you can reach. I believe that we all have a function, a purpose, a job to do in this life. The day we know for sure what we want to do in the world is the day that our past and our future come together with clarity. We can put the past with its experiences into proper perspective as training to reach this point. Then we can plan and shape the road before us with specific goals in mind. Educational choices, relations, travel, and training become steps along the path to success.

When we know where we are going and doing what we love, our hearts, spirits, and minds become unified in purpose. Figuring out the next step is a joy because you know you are on the right path. And even if every day is not rosy, and they will not be, you can see the bigger picture and mount the courage and fortitude to press on and lean into the life you desire.

Once we know why we are here, we can get busy fulfilling the purpose of our life as we understand it now. I believe we are here for one reason, and that is to serve our Creator and be the best we can be. We belong to God. One day, we will resurrect and return to the Sustainer of the universe.

12. TRUST

"The only way to know if you can trust somebody is to trust them."

ERNEST HEMMINGWAY

In a world where it seems as though all we hear about and see is how one person betrayed another, how do we allow ourselves to trust someone to get close at all, let alone trust them to be near the most fragile parts of us? We expect to be told the truth. We anticipate that others will not be dishonest. We place our hopes in others and, in doing so, it leaves us vulnerable.

Imagine having spent your entire life having to watch your back literally and figuratively, not just because there are strangers who may want to harm you, but also because even those who are supposed to be close to you could turn against you in an instant. Perhaps you've spent most of your career in a profession where you are constantly exposed to negative human behavior. You've observed trauma and are constantly under high-stress situations that impact your ability to trust others. The environment that you spend time in can contribute to difficulties building and maintaining trust.

We each come to crossroads in our lives where we must make the decision to let go of our old survival mechanisms to grow and make room for something better. Sometimes what used to protect us becomes what harms us and stifles the capacity for our lives to be open and full of joy, love, and peace.

When it comes to trusting each other, we must accept that our past is not our present. We must be able to recognize that what hurt us before is not necessarily what is currently standing before us, even when the situation looks frighteningly similar, and sometimes even when it's the same person. Does this mean we won't ever get hurt again? No. That's a part of life. People will let us down, and we will let them down, but that doesn't mean our efforts to disassemble our defense mechanisms are in vain.

If we never allow ourselves any vulnerability, we lose out on the opportunity to make incredibly deep and meaningful connections that open our lives in ways we couldn't experience any other way. Those connections draw out the very best within and create a new reality, one where we learn that the only way to know if you can believe somebody is honest is to have faith in them.

13. TRANQUILITY

> "In the midst of hate, I found there was within me an invincible love. In the midst of chaos, I found there was within me an invincible calm."

ALBERT CAMUS

During your tranquil moments is when you find your true meaning. Amid those peaceful junctures is when you become inviolable and unbending. It is in those serene and undisturbed stages of your life that you become dauntless and impregnable.

I discovered that within me there was a hidden smile amid tears. I found within myself a beautiful summer during a brutal winter. Joy fills my heart knowing that no matter how difficult the world can be and how challenging life can become, within me there is something stronger pushing right back.

The moment we learn who we truly are is when the world pushes against us. When the universe provokes us and dares us to commit, we find the reason for our existence. We learn to withstand and resist. Despite everything we experience, we are a powerful thought conjured by the Omnipotent God, built to conquer any problem and defeat any complication.

Even with the darkness consuming me, there is an invincible light that pierces through. A relaxing calm rises without warning as my soul rises above the chaos.

In those complex, intricate, and impenetrable thoughts, a mysterious power gets me through the day. I have faith that it will take me through both the good and difficult times of life. And I am thankful to God for that.

14. ONCE UPON A TIME

"There was a time above, a time before, there were perfect things, diamond absolutes. But things fall, things on earth. And what falls, is fallen. In the dream, it took me to the light. A beautiful lie."

SILENT GUARDIAN

Reading these words, I flash back to when I was young, reminiscing about my past and feeling the urge to tell others how I feel. What followed was sadness and anger from my traumas and obsessions. And I know why. Before my traumatic experience, I was a happy, joyful child. My life wasn't perfect, but it felt like heaven, and I thought it would last forever.

Suddenly and unfortunately, my life took a tragic turn. I experienced a traumatic event, and I couldn't do anything to prevent it from happening. More importantly, after it happened, I couldn't do anything to avoid my bad experience. Have you endured something traumatic in your life? Has that experience made you prone to heightened anxiety, depression or emotional numbness?

What falls, is fallen. What dies stays that way. I was broken and angry. Why did it happen? Perhaps the Lord knows why. I can only assume that this is life on Earth. Imperfect, faulty, not forever-lasting. Unfortunate things can happen anytime, and they can't be undone. Humans are mortal, and that's their biggest flaw. It leads to all the other flaws a person can have. A beautiful lie can provide temporary comfort, but it often stands in the way of genuine healing and self-understanding. It's challenging to confront the painful truth we avoid, while also acknowledging that the lies we tell ourselves may have served a purpose—offering survival in moments of deep vulnerability.

My traumatic experience scarred me, and I have been forever wounded. A broken person, a lost soul with demons, but when you confront your fears, you are freed from them. It dawned on me that I could become better—that I could be stronger, endure loss, and rebuild. I finally had my faith in humanity restored. Then, just as I thought I had turned the corner, I was greeted by a deceptive gleam. Everything I believed about love was a lie, and everything I had ever known was shattered. But then I remembered that love is a virtue, and all gifts are from God.

15. SERENITY

"Never be in a hurry; do everything quietly and in a calm spirit. Do not lose your inner peace for anything whatsoever, even if your whole world seems upset."

FRANCIS DE SALES

Bask in the waters that illuminate a waterfall. Sit where the sun's rays will rise. Listen to nature's call. Hear the calm of the wind and see the dances of the trees. Feel the stillness in the air as it brings you a state of inner peace and tranquility. Don't rush. Never force anything. Stay composed. Never stray toward the path of unrest. Your peace is important to you and others. Serenity is far more important than what you seek. You will face troubles on your journey. Complications will greet you, but be strong. Have courage. Know that you are destined to be important, and your hardships will be rewarded.

When your tasks are completed in silence, your appreciation will thrive. When you don't seek others' validation, your labor will be respected. When your life becomes nothing but troubles, worry, and distress, know that the Almighty will always be there to comfort you. When you allow your Lord to guide you, only then will you experience true inner peace and a calm spirit.

Learn to pay attention when your spirit is inwardly troubled. Frustrations can come from feelings of injustice or lack of control. Let go of your attachments and strive to maintain equanimity. Prevent everyday obstacles from overpowering you. Before an issue triggers your anger, try to reduce the intensity of the angry feelings by calming yourself. God enable us to have peace within, in spite of the suffering we go through and the storms that rage around us.

Have faith that during pressing times, you do not need to be afraid. When the universe is upset, nourish it with peace and harmony. Focus on the present moment and accept your thoughts and feelings. Be just and balanced in your actions and don't let setbacks make you feel disheartened. Don't give up too quickly because your Lord knows what's best for you.

16. PRAISEWORTHY

"There is none worthy of worship but your Lord."

HOLY QURAN, 9:31

The belief in the Supreme God is the center of most people's faith. Some believe in the existence of many gods, others believe there is no god, and then there are those who believe that the existence or nonexistence of a god or of gods is unknown or unknowable. The declaration that 'there is no one worthy of worship except one God' is the oneness of God. Being the only Creator, Preserver, and Nourisher, your Lord oversees all creation. He created the universe and has power over everything within it. He is exalted above everything He creates, and His greatness cannot be compared to His creation.

One must acknowledge that it is God alone who deserves to be worshipped and thus abstain from worshipping any other thing or being. None is equal to Him. He is God of all humankind, not of a special tribe or race. Having achieved this knowledge of the One True God, one should constantly have faith in Him and allow nothing to induce them to deny the truth. When true faith enters a person's heart, it impacts the person's outlook and behavior.

No matter what your belief is, we must respect all religions. We must respect all faiths and be kind to all credence. We may have our differences but, in the end, only the Lord can judge us. Because everyone is created by God Almighty, the Maker of all, humans must treat one another with honor, respect, and loving kindness. Be good to one another and live in peace and harmony, for you shall see the rewards that your Lord promised you.

17. SELFLESS

*"I give waters in the wilderness and rivers in
the desert, to give drink to my people."*

HOLY BIBLE, 43:20

When you pass through the inhospitable parts of life to praise your Lord, He gives you water to quench your thirst. The illusion begins when you fail to comprehend His greatness, showering His grace upon you. Your Lord wants to refresh and comfort your heart. He is the only one you shall honor and glorify.

There have been many dark and difficult days in my life. Fierce enemies came from every direction, and anguish and heartache were felt on many occasions, but now God gives me rest from the battles, just as He promised. It was a long journey, and my dedication was put to the test. The Lord always remembers my heart, and I was assured of His faithfulness when I was told. The Lord will never leave me, and I find peace and rest in this promise.

Life brings circumstances that make it difficult to remember the Lord's promise, but I pray you will never lose sight of His love and care for you. Humankind tends to be distracted and guided by the world. We must ask the Lord to bend our hearts to Him so that we will live in ways that are pleasing to Him. Within us, there is a rebellious nature, so we ask the Lord to incline our hearts to Him so that we will submit to His will. God will never give you more than you can handle.

Selflessness is rooted in compassion, empathy, and pri-oritizing other's needs. God encourages believers to wish goodness for others as they would for themselves. Our prayers must be unselfish and made with a pure heart. As God blesses us, may those divine gifts bless other people and bend their hearts toward Him. May peace be upon you, my friend.

18. THE TUNNEL

"Whatever dark tunnel we may be called upon to travel through, God has been there."

ELISABETH ELLIOT

No matter what challenges I have endured, God has always been with me. With every pain and disappointment, God has watched over me. I may not know it, but His supreme plan for me is in the making. I am bursting with a new-found feeling of my own existence, with strong and powerful frequencies. My mind wanders to wide open fields and long-forgotten lands with limitless possibilities. I am not quite there yet.

Holding still in anticipation, I don't want to miss hearing my inner voice, soft and deep. With me are friendly skies on rainy days and my life is getting warmer. Walk through that tunnel. No matter how frightening it may be, know that you'll make it through. Faith will cross you over to the other side. Walk to the light as the sloping tunnel walls circulate around you. Is the promising beacon getting closer?

During my walk through the famed Cypress Tree Tunnel at Point Reyes, California, I observed trees arching over, creating an ethereal tunnel effect. My mind immediately thought about the tunnels that our life journeys go through and how faith plays a significant role in the decisions we make. The trees were erected there as if God ordered them to stand perfectly in the shape of an underpass. As the trees block the light of the sun, darkness slowly creeps in. But as you walk farther into the tunnel, the light of God is observed. A beacon of hope flickers, persuading the unfortunate to come near. And only through faith do we continue to move forward as the light shines upon our soul.

There will be times when you want to turn around. There will be moments when you doubt your destination. You will want to give up. Keep walking, because the beauty of life is only experienced through heartbreak and disappointment. When that dark tunnel ends, the blessing of your being will resonate with the cosmos.

19. REVERENCE

"Pursue some path, however narrow and crooked, in which you can walk with love and reverence."

HENRY DAVID THOREAU

Some paths in our lives speak to us. They may not be a direct route, but rather circuitous. They take us from relatively tame, somewhat predictable suburbia to adventures beyond our wildest dreams. My activities are often too implausible and hard to describe to someone with a more mainstream perspective. I am learning that the absence of peaks and valleys can be rather boring. I choose the road less traveled without the benefit of a compass or roadmap, except that which is firmly lodged in my heart.

I often use the power of God, trusting that it will show me where I need to go. It has led me, without exception,

There are lessons we can only understand in a storm. It's easy to be grateful when things are going well, but we can find things to be grateful for even in difficulty. Stopping to look for God's good hand and keeping a daily gratitude list helps us see that God is at work all around us, even when circumstances are hard.

Some trials bring us to the end of ourselves. In those times, we realize we're completely dependent on God. We need Him to give us wisdom, to replace our fear with faith, and to give us strength to battle the storm. But that's a good place to be. God designed us to be utterly dependent on Him.

As I was paddling my canoe down the Colorado River in Arizona, it reminded me of life and how beautiful the journey to faith can be. But in a split second, the calm waters could've turned tumultuous. Do I cling to the shore or continue to sail? As my canoe glided along the running water, I realized that life will always continue, through injustice and the feelings of predation and instinct. Life will swallow you up if you remain constant. Always paddle your way to bigger and better things. The more you grow, the more you will realize the power of your potential.

None of us are immune from the storms of life. While we don't know how or when they will hit, God has assured us they will come. It's a reminder that this world is not our home. This world is temporary, and your constant struggle to attain peace will one day be granted. Paddle away in the endless sea of life, as the Lord promises that your struggles and hard work will one day be rewarded.

22. THE WIND

"If you reveal your secrets to the wind, you should not blame the wind for revealing them to the trees."

KHALIL GIBRAN

The wind leaves no trails. When a secret is revealed, it will travel with the wind and to its destination. After a night of howling wind, broken branches obstruct the path to the truth. It's a reminder of the casualties of the wind's violent pummeling. The leafy top of a tree acts like a sail, and the force on the tree as it is caught by gusts of strong wind is enormous. Yet those splintered boughs are the exception, since most trees manage to withstand the storm. The secret to this resilience is that trees sway when pushed.

It's true that a friend today can be an enemy tomorrow. But an enemy can also become a friend. As much as we want to keep secrets, in the end, it is truly out of our hands when it comes to who knows our treasures and who knows our sorrows. Most people have secrets of some kind. What makes some people want to tell their secrets and others continue to hide them? People often reveal secrets because it is cathartic or makes them feel better, which can improve their health.

Keeping a secret requires a great deal of effort and decision making. The communication strategies that people use to reveal their secrets reflect these decisions. God is aware of everything people do in secret and will judge and reward them accordingly. However, there are some things hidden from us, and these secrets belong to the Lord. The secret of God is with those who fear Him, and He will show them His covenant. Remember that if your secrets cannot be kept safe with your fellow humans, the secret between you and your Lord will always remain sealed.

23. FINGERPRINT

"Wherever love is found, that is the place where God lives."

DARLA EVANS

Your fingerprint is unique. No two fingerprints are alike, which is mind blowing. From the order and complexity found in the universe and in living creatures, philosophers and theologians have reached the conclusion that God exists. This is known as the design argument.

Evidence of design can be found as far away as the most distant stars and as close as the palm of your hand. Familiar and seemingly simple, the human hand is a marvel of functional utility and complexity that provides powerful evidence for the existence of God. If God did indeed design the human hand, why do we have fingerprints? Do they perform a function, and if not, then why would God have created us with them?

Our fingerprints help us to feel objects through vibrations. As you move your fingers across a surface, you trigger vibrations that are picked up by your nerves. Some of these nerves are embedded relatively deep, yet our sense of touch is so refined that we can feel textural differences as small as the width of a human hair.

Like a fingerprint, everyone's relationship with God is unique and different and no connection is alike. God is love, and whoever lives in love lives in God. Love is made complete amongst us so that we will have confidence on judgment day. Love is a sacred, divine force, and understanding or experiencing true love is akin to comprehending and becoming familiar with God. He is the center point and the originator of true love. He is the true foundation of lasting love and something that cannot be forced upon another. It is through faith that we can love.

24. THE SEA

*"You cried when He took away your drop of water,
not knowing He'd saved for you the sea."*

YASMIN MOGAHED

How often we wish we could turn back the hands of time and start over. We will endure many situations in life where we lose our most precious moments. Have you ever realized that you wasted your youth because you felt lost and had no one to guide you? Have you ever invested so much time and effort in a relationship only to have it disappear because of a misunderstanding? When these losses occur, it takes tremendous faith to trust the Lord. Yes, things can be painful and difficult, but God will never leave us empty. He will replace everything we lost. If He asks us to put something down, it's because He wants us to pick up something greater.

Just because God didn't answer your prayers doesn't mean He's not listening. He just has something better in store for you. You might have lost your job, a beautiful relationship, or something valuable. It might be tearing you apart, especially when you have no idea what God has in store for you. Those months and years you have waited are never in vain. With this promise, remember that God will never take something away from you without the intention of replacing it with something much better.

Most of us don't realize how merciful God has been to us despite our sinful ways. Anytime we talk about blessings, we tend to think about finances. If God opens your eyes to see the troubles that await you or the path you take, I don't think you would ever come out of your house again, but He said never to be afraid when He is helping you. It's time to trust God because He will never stop helping you. If God takes away something you never expected to lose, He can replace it with something you never expected to have.

25. MISTAKES

> *"In order for the light to shine so brightly,*
> *the darkness must be present."*

FRANCIS BACON

Sometimes negative things or situations happen to bring us back to our destiny. You might have been hurt, but the person who hurt you may not have meant to cause you sorrow. You might have been rejected, but that's not the end of your life. You have been waiting for so long to start a career, a family, or trusting God for something. The moon and the stars shine in their own time. Maybe you must see the dark before you can appreciate the light.

When faith goes dark, the senses fail. When the sun

hides and things are hidden in the shadow, prayers vanish. It's as though the eyes fail and the heart fears. Although others may point to the beams of light, everything appears like dusk. The practice of prayer used to connect to God can dry up. The feeling of love may grow cold and quiet. Affirming the things you believe can be difficult, but I can tell you that God has not forsaken you. Just as the night is not the end of the sun, your faith will also not end by the dark hour. Never disengage. Remain in the company of those who will believe in you and will pray while you are silent.

We must see the good things that happen in our life as miracles and the unfortunate moments as divine. Life itself is a gift of many miracles. Don't let little things or worry take away your hope. Have faith and keep believing that someday, somewhere, your time of celebration will come.

For years, I have been walking under a cloud of uncertainty. I prayed and held firm in my faith that things would eventually turn my way. Pain and suffering can be a result of wrong behaviors, but God forgives many mistakes. When we accept that an error in judgment has been made, we repent. In doing so, we learn and grow wiser. Mistakes can be catalysts for self-improvement and a great way to ensure we do not follow our thoughts and desires. Remember to never forget your mistakes but instead learn from them and grow your faith in God.

26. THE INVISIBLE

"Everything is laid out for you. Your path is straight ahead of you. Sometimes it's invisible, but it's there."

CHIEF LEON SHENANDOAH

Most people will never find the right path and spend their lives surrounded by the wrong people and doing things they don't enjoy. Today, it's particularly easy to get confused as to what we want in life since we are constantly told by friends and our culture what we should be like, what we should do, and how we should look. Still, there are individuals who don't conform to what the majority wants and listen to the voices of their own souls.

Finding your path is not an act of searching. It is an act of allowing. When you let go of what you think should be, you allow what is meant to be. Maybe you held on to someone or something too long, hoping for better. Maybe that absence has made you a better person, even when you don't believe so.

Simply follow your heart moment by moment. Your purpose is already built into your being. When you follow your heart, your inner map, you will be nudged in the right direction. Because what finding your path comes down to is living life to the fullest. It comes down to following what makes you feel alive and doing your best in this moment. You may not know where your path is going, but you have to follow the road. It's the path to the Creator. That's the only path there is. May your path be gentle and kind.

27. CHAOS

"In the chaotic rage that fuels my soul, there is a relaxing calm that rises without warning."

DARK NIGHT BEACON

Even with temper consuming me, there is a hidden beacon that pierces through. In the chaotic rage that fuels my soul, there is a relaxing calm that rises without warning. To get past my dark moments, I must know myself better and be open to internal work. I must become aware of what doesn't work and never give up on myself. I must appreciate the dark with the mindset that dawn is near.

Chaos in the world is a test and is meant to challenge you and help you grow. Disorder is intended to increase your faith. In times of distress and loss, we are reminded of the importance of peace and righteousness. We must pray for our brethren and be grateful for what we are provided. When your trust in the Lord is solidified, only then will we understand the miracles of hardship.

Your symbol, your identity, must rise. You must leave your mark. Your image will reveal your character. In doing so, you realize you'll soon overcome your obstacles. In those complex, intricate, and impenetrable thoughts, there is a mysterious power that gets you through the day. You have faith that it will guide you through the good and difficult times of life. And you thank God for that.

28. MYSTERY

> *"There's a universe inside your head—a place of pictures and passions, of songs and sorrows. It's everything you are—and it's an utter mystery."*

JEFFREY KLUGER

The universe exists in your conscious experience, in the depths of your mind. Just as our bodies are cells in the body of the universe, our consciousness is immersed in the universal mind. Nature has allowed us to enter our mental universe only to discover the infinitude of the conscious universe. Infinity is hard to think about, but happily, our brains keep evolving. We see incredible mathematical orderliness in our cosmos, and we've reached the horizon where reality may reveal its true source.

Your memory plays an essential role in your daily life. On the surface, pulling up memories may seem simple, but the process for forming and storing them is complex because of all the activity in your brain. There is a universe inside all of us. A place where we grow and experience life. A place we eventually return to. It is in this vast space where we store our lives. From heartbreak to joy, from excitement to mourning.

But in the depths of our universe hides a mystery that we do not know of. Like the abyss, its beautiful darkness conceals our true identity. In our journey of life, we struggle to find this missing piece of us. Our souls know it's a place we will eventually go to, but it is not yet ready to be discovered. It's a place of hope, a place of faith, and a place of reliance where you are encouraged by the Lord to use logic, reasoning, and intellect.

29. THE STAR

*"And it is He who placed for you the stars that
you may be guided by them through the
darknesses of the land and sea."*

HOLY QURAN, 6:97

In the constellation Scutum, there is a star so massive, it is considered the biggest star ever discovered in the universe. With an approximate distance of 19,570 light years from Earth, the immense size is not only unimaginable but very difficult to comprehend. The star, Stephenson 2-18, is a member of a class of stars known as hypergiants, and it's about 2,150 times the Sun's radius, over seven billion times larger than our Sun.

Stars are born within clouds of dust and scattered throughout most galaxies. Turbulence deep within these clouds gives rise to knots with sufficient mass where the gas and dust can begin to collapse under its own gravitational attraction. As the cloud collapses, the material at the center heats up. It is this hot core at the heart of the collapsing cloud that becomes a star over millions of years.

I find it useful to think about life as the physical expression of the person I have been. Because we change in our mind and heart at a faster rate than the physical world allows for, the life we are confronting, like a star, is an expression of the past. If we construct our lives to express our future self, there should be a moment when we become that person we've always wanted to be. Then we can look in the mirror of our lives and see a true reflection of who we are at that very moment.

When the night covered you in darkness, a star was placed for you so that you may be guided. Each star is a point of light in the heavens, a beacon for a lost soul in the desert or a lonely mariner on the high seas. Knowledge of these laws empowers humankind to chart its course during journeys on earth and in the vast expanse of space. May your journey in life be as bright as the star of your dreams.

30. THE GREAT VOID

"So verily, I swear by the stars that are veiled. And by the sweeping stars that move swiftly and hide themselves. Verily, this is the Word of your Lord."

HOLY QURAN, 15-19

In the constellation Pheonix, there is a black hole so massive, it is considered the biggest black hole ever discovered in the universe. With an approximate distance of 8.6 billion light years from Earth, its size is inconceivable. Phoenix A, a supermassive black hole, with a mass of one hundred billion suns is so huge that it could engulf the entire Solar System without blinking. Its mass and size are a true behemoth.

We will never be able to comprehend a black hole, with its immense power and mystery. They are formed when a star that has consumed all its fuel collapses in itself, eventually turning into a black hole with infinite density and zero volume and an immensely powerful magnetic field. We are unable to see black holes, even with the most powerful telescope, because their gravitational pull is so strong that light is unable to escape from its gargantuan grasp. However, such a collapsed star can be perceived by means of the effect it has on the surrounding area.

A black hole may consume everything into nothing, but it does not mean it is gone forever. Every moment God creates, and every exact detail of the universe are created in and destined for eternity. They do not die or vanish. Everything we can imagine will endure for eternity, a notion that cannot be fully comprehended.

Only those who truly seek the guidance of their Lord and endeavor to appreciate His infinite might and His greatness will heed these mysteries and have a grasp of the unknown. Appreciate the vastness of the universe, for the Lord is the creator of all creations. He wants to humble you, to bring you closer to His mercy and forgiveness. Always have faith; its power will guide you during life's challenges and help you find purpose, cultivate hope, and foster a sense of peace during your life's supernova.

CHAPTER IV

LOVE

Live a life where you feel everything. Let love sting you deep. Let the joy and pain of every emotion touch your soul. When you love, you'll also find God. He lurks in the depths of affection, in the curves of fondness, and in the corner of tenderness. The Almighty is found between devotion and adoration. He is as close to you as your fingerprints and as near to you as your heart. Learn to love with all your heart and painfully let go to show your true affection. Love is based on affection and mercy. No other feeling has the power to bind, heal, and propel us toward our greatest potential.

1. COMMUNICATION

"Between what is said and not meant, and what is meant and not said, most of love is lost."

KHALIL GIBRAN

The biggest barrier in love is communication. What is considered by one as less insignificant can be considered very significant to the other, which leads to dispute in the relationship. There is a lot of unspoken love in relationships, but pride, ego, past hurts, and stubbornness make it impossible to voice. Even people who live under the same roof drift further and further away from each other, and love is lost.

Every time you're about to insult someone, I want you to find something to love about them instead. It might go against every instinct you have. Love can and does get lost all the time in this world. We wonder why the message can be misunderstood, but most love is lost because we make assumptions.

Maybe it's a couple in the heat of an intense argument who say things they can't take back because they're hurt, and they want the other person to hurt as much as they do. Maybe it's something as simple as letting relationships slide with our friends and family across the bridges of time and distance.

Tell people you appreciate your time together, how they've impacted your life, and what they mean to you. Send a message to those who have drifted away from you. Perhaps you can mend the friendship even though the two of you may have moved on. You only have one life, and to forgive is beautiful. In that beauty sits the presence of peace. You may decide not to play the love dance ever again, but you have learned that love is not always intended in the way it's supposed to. Sometimes what is uttered may signal the end or the beginning of something magical, even in solitude.

2. THE INEVITABLE

"I knew from the beginning that I have found you to lose you, and I loved you to miss you. We met in coincidence, and we were two arrows with opposite directions, and inevitable were the meeting and the farewell."

GHADA AL SAMMAN

The concept of a meeting that coincides with an inevitable farewell in love carries a poignant mix of fate and melancholy. It's like a love story fated to begin and end almost simultaneously, filled with intensity because both parties may sense the fleeting nature of their connection. This is one of the reasons why we must always live in the moment, cherishing each second despite the knowledge that it might soon be over.

When two people meet at a time when circumstances guarantee they cannot stay together, but the strength of their attraction pulls them toward each other anyway, their love burns brightly but briefly, leaving lasting impressions that outlive the relationship. The emotional rollercoaster of hope and euphoria while finding love to sorrow and resignation of having to let it go can be daunting. The knowledge of an impending end can also make each moment more intense, more fragile.

Inevitable loss carries a profound sense of emotional weight. It touches on the transient nature of human connections, the vulnerability that comes with loving deeply, and the pain of knowing that nothing, even the most intense relationships, can last forever. When love fades, it will still leave a lasting imprint.

If you have been through a separation, you know it hurts. It changes you. The feeling of being certain and unable to avoid a breakup is stressful. But you must realize that God's will is stronger than any chance, any luck, and any plan. The journey of love is never perfect and unfortunately not always kind. Every heart is in God's hand, and perhaps the love you were seeking is within.

3. THE HEART

"There are hearts that won't ever hate you, no matter how much you hurt them."

MAHMOUD DARWISH

Some hearts know only love. No matter how much they are hurt, broken, or neglected, they will always return endearment. You can try to lie to them. You can harm or sabotage them, but they will always find a way to show you devotion. The more pain you give them, the more passion they will return. Treasure these hearts. Love them. Take good care of them. Do not take advantage of them. They are a blessing from God. These hearts don't come often. They understand only compassion. Little do people know that these hearts have already been through distress, suffering, grief, and misery. They have encountered anguish, agony, sadness, and sorrow.

This type of love is filled with emotional complexity and tension. The agony of loving someone who not only doesn't love you but resents or despises you can be explored as a form of emotional martyrdom. The love becomes self-sacrificial, knowing it may never be returned. The dynamics of unreciprocated love and devotion are not for the soft hearted.

Kindness is a mark of faith and a sign of love. Whoever dismisses hate and expresses endearment is highly valued. Your love should be all-encompassing and how you spread your kindness to others is an act of genuine nourishment. If someone shows hatred, display an act of love. Understand them. Learn from them and appreciate them. Most importantly, love them dearly because they will always love you back, no matter how upset at you they may be. Remember that they do not live forever. Take time to understand them because no heart will love you in the same way they can. If you're wondering how you can find such angels in this world, simply look at the love your parents have for you.

4. RESPECT

"Do not leave yourself to find someone else."

RUNE LAZULI

Sometimes, when you lose someone, you realize you forgot who you were in your own right. Remember that no one can truly love you until you love yourself. Not everyone has a good heart. Not everyone has good intentions. Not everyone displays good faith. Never give up on your dreams unless someone is a part of that dream—through thick and thin, good and bad, for better or worse, despite all obstacles and supporting in all circumstances.

You wanted nothing but to be with them. You would've gone out of your way to find them and keep them. In doing so, you were slowly losing yourself. You forgot who you were. Your judgment became impaired. You chased what no longer wanted to stay. Remember that you can be there for others, but never leave yourself behind because the one person you will never lose is yourself. No other act of self-love is holy, and no other intention of self-care is comparable.

Are you waiting for that person to find you? Only you know who you are and who you want to be with. Do not abandon yourself for someone else. Only you understand yourself and the things you want. Only you know what makes you genuinely happy. Give yourself the kind of love that will satisfy your soul because you are the only one who knows what you deserve.

5. THE DREAM

> *"I avoided you by sleeping and you*
> *welcomed me in my first dream."*

NIZAR QABBANI

Seeing someone you used to love in a dream when you're actively trying to forget or avoid them brings a powerful tension between the conscious and subconscious mind.

Dreams often act as a space where unresolved emotions surface despite attempts to suppress them in waking life. This can evoke a mix of emotions—sadness, longing, confusion, and even frustration—because the dream reopens a door you've worked hard to close.

Have you tried moving on and realized that even past love can haunt you in your dreams? It can serve as a reminder that, no matter how much time passes, some connections leave a mark that can't easily be erased. The mind may hold onto unresolved feelings, and this dream encounter might symbolize unfinished emotional business. Perhaps it could signify that part of you is still holding on, even if you believe you've let go. The dream could be a manifestation of unresolved guilt, loss, or nostalgia.

The dream may ultimately serve as a moment of emotional release. You're trying to avoid thinking about the person, but the dream forces you to confront your feelings, possibly leading to acceptance or a greater understanding of why they're struggling to move on.

This is the description of a person who chooses to forget someone by sleeping in order to ease the pain in their heart. Although it may work for a little while, eventually the love is too deep to be suppressed and in return, their yearning grows stronger. As difficult as it may seem, learn to let go, but appreciate that space in your heart for the love that was never meant to be.

6. BONDING

"Most of all, I'm scared of walking out of this room and never feeling the rest of my whole life the way I feel when I am with you."

JENNIFER GREY

Have you ever felt a special bond with someone? A bond so powerful that you know you could not ignore it. A feeling that you have never felt before, a once-in-a-lifetime affection. Did you have to make a choice whether to be with or without them?

Some of you might have been in a situation where you were afraid to leave that room, that moment, that place because you knew you would never feel that special feeling again. You would never smell that scent. You would never see those eyes, that gaze, that smile. You would never hear their voice or feel their touch, the warmth of their love. You knew that if you turned your back, you would never see them again.

The clock doesn't stop for anyone or anything. Appreciate every moment because opportunities do not come often. Confront your fear and take the chance you have been dreaming about. You may never get another shot at your aspirations or to express your true emotions to those you hold dear in your heart.

I urge you to never give up—through thick and thin, through the peaks and valleys, for better or worse, despite all obstacles and with support in all circumstances. You will one day regret walking away, and it will haunt you for the rest of your life.

7. WISDOM

*"You are my beginning and ending, and every sad,
happy, hard, easy, beautiful moment in between."*

DARK NIGHT BEACON

It's not every day that you meet someone who will inspire you; Who will change you. Some wait a lifetime, while others never get the chance to meet them. An opportunity to greet a person who will change your thoughts and alter your mind in a beautiful way does not come frequently. This person will motivate, influence, galvanize, and stir your heart. They will give rise to your intimate side. And most importantly, they will awaken your soul. If you are fortunate to have met this person, they may also unfortunately be taken away from you for many reasons. It will hurt you to your soul. You will miss them dearly.

Perhaps you're missing someone dear to you. You miss them on their birthday and all those times they made you feel special. You miss the feeling you had when you first met them. You miss the emotions you had when they first looked at you. The first date at a coffee shop as you became mesmerized by their beautiful eyes, by the touch of their hand and the warmth of their hugs; Or their sweet scent and feel of their hair. You will miss seeing their beautiful face and the kindness they had in their heart. They were your beginning and will always be your ending. Every sad, happy, hard, easy, and beautiful moment you endured with them was a blessing. And for that, you can never thank them enough.

Walking away can be one the hardest choices, but it can also be an act of profound love and strength. This wisdom grows from recognizing when love is no longer nourishing, when it requires you to sacrifice your well-being or personal growth. It involves accepting that not every love story is meant to last forever, and sometimes the best thing you can do is let go. You hope their smile will always be great. You hope their lovely eyes always see the best in others. You aspire that their kind heart always has peace. You will miss them, and you hope they will miss you too.

8. RELINQUISHMENT

"If you love something, set it free. If it comes back, it's yours. If not, it was never meant to be."

UNKNOWN

The struggle of sacrifice has been with humanity since the beginning of time. Going out of our comfort zone and doing what's best for others is a difficult task. We are creatures of survival, and we hold on to what we find dear because it makes us feel safe. However, to have the best quality of life, we sometimes need to make sacrifices in order to be happier, and if it works out, then great. If not, then it wasn't meant to be.

When distance grows with someone we love, we may feel like we should bargain for them to return. We may try talking to them and negotiate or beg for forgiveness. If the two of you love each other, then the fight won't be enough to end things. However, if they don't love you enough, they won't make any effort to fix things.

It's understandable that you wouldn't want a relationship to end. You may feel the person is the best you've ever had, and if you let them go, you might not be able to find someone better. This is certainly a risk, but if the relationship is falling apart, perhaps you should let it go, if only temporarily. Friends do drift apart with time. Work, family commitments, school, and life can make people stop talking. Good friends continue to have a bond even if time has pulled them apart. When the two of you do talk again, it will be like no time has passed.

Love gives without expectations. Love sets everything it touches free. Only fate can determine whether a relationship was meant to be. If you let someone go, they will come back if that's your destiny. But you cannot force someone to love you. You must give them the freedom to choose. Letting someone go can be difficult, but it's not impossible. By doing so, you can show someone how much you truly love them, knowing you may never have them again.

9. FOREVER

"I will forever wish you the best, even though it was me you no longer chose to love. I will forever think you're magic, even though it's not me that will embrace your charm."

DARK NIGHT BEACON

Wishing someone the best in their absence is the purest form of love. Wish them the best with all your heart, no matter what caused your unraveling. You'll never forget them. Maybe life brought the two of you waves of mistrust and deception, and you lost them in that ocean. You tried to pull them back, but they drifted away. One day the thoughts will eat you up too much to continue thinking back on the good times.

Have you struggled to cope with a loss and finally decided it was time to let go of the monster growing inside you? Feeding off your hatred of what couldn't be changed, you began to detach yourself from love's strong magnetic forces. After crying yourself to sleep thinking about them, the closure you needed was to contact them again and see how they were doing. You needed to send them one last wish goodbye. With that, you were able to relinquish the anger clinging to your soul.

The two of you will never get back together, and that's okay. You can still love them for the memories you shared and wish them the best in finding out who they are and learning to become a better, healthier, and more honest individual in hopes of finding their happiness.

Love is not a whip used to keep someone down. It's a selfless gift we can only give to each other when we realize it's a rarity in its raw and genuine form. No matter how the relationship ended, no matter who they're with now, no matter the differences we have.

When you put all that aside and recognize that they were once your best friend, it's easier to remember what nurtured your bond. You forgive them and wish them well, and your heart will feel so much lighter. Forgiveness is the first step to healing this aching heart of yours forever. You can move forward by letting someone go who doesn't want to stay because it is your ultimate gift of love that will peacefully bridge the gap of the loss.

10. THE PRETENDER

"May you never steal, lie, or cheat, but if you must steal, then steal away my sorrows, and if you must lie, lie with me all the nights of my life, and if you must cheat, then please cheat death because I couldn't live a day without you."

DOMINIQUE MCELLIGOTT

Have you loved someone so much that you hoped they would never loot and never take away something that did not belong to them? Did you hope they would never falsify and always honor the truth? You hoped they would never deceive and would always remain true. But, when necessary, you hoped they would raid your misery and take all the pain away. You hoped they could fabricate a way to devote every day of their life to you. You knew it wasn't possible, but if they could make you believe they'd always be by your side, it would bring you peace. And you hoped they would elude death because you couldn't live without them.

If you were married or in a serious relationship, you wanted to dedicate your life to them. A connection long before the two of you ever met bound you together. You promised to encourage and inspire them, to laugh with them, and to comfort them in times of sorrow and struggle. And if they were no longer present for any reason, you wanted your memories to leave them a constant reminder of your endearment, even if faith chose a different path for the two of you.

But if they were here, you would promise to love them in good times and in bad, when life seemed easy and when it seemed hard, when their love was simple and when it was an effort. You would promise to cherish them and to always hold them in the highest regard. These things you would give to them today and all the days until the end of your life.

So, wherever they go, whatever they do, you will be right here waiting for them. And whatever it takes or how your heart breaks, you will be right here waiting for them. You will always be waiting just for them.

11. PRESERVATION

"Some hearts will never give up on you."

DARK NIGHT BEACON

It's true that some hearts will never surrender. They will never deny their love. They will refuse to back down. Even though storms of misunderstanding shake the ocean of your friendship, they will be there holding on as if their mere existence depends on it. They are unwilling to allow any expanse of sadness, whether brief or ongoing, to cut apart the string that binds the two of you. It means they are aware and not dismissive. They are painted by the powerful inspiration of your character.

There will be days when they ignore you. Don't take ignorance for hate. It's just that they don't want to dwell in the nostalgia of the shattered utopia anymore. When they go quiet, know that they are also feeling the pain of separation. Even though you forgot to remember that they, too, had collapsed by the inevitability of falling into the abyss of grief before evoking the guilt in them for not holding your most frail fragments. And still, they will not give up on you. For they are stuck between the art of trying harder and letting go. They will swallow every feeling of resentment you give them in the hopes that they can triumph with their emotions ablaze.

It's how you write the story in between that makes all the difference. They want a story filled with love, so they will set their ego aside. They know the journey won't be easy because in life, nothing meaningful is easy. You may leave them with scars and a bruised, abandoned heart, but they will never give up on you, and that is because their mere existence depends on you.

The perspective of never giving up on love involves resilience—the ability to face heartbreak, disappointment, or loss, and keep an open heart. It is understood that love is not a singular, unchanging entity but something that evolves, takes different forms, and can be found in unexpected places. You can also extend this concept to loving oneself, recognizing that the journey to maintaining love with another often starts from within.

12. THE LONGING

"I have to remind myself that some birds aren't meant to be caged. Their feathers are just too bright."

STEPHEN KING

When the person you most revere flies away, part of you knows it was a sin to lock them away. You feel as if your love confined them to the point where they were no longer free. Perhaps your adoration was too much. Your heart and the place you call home is dull and empty now that they're gone. Does the feeling of missing your friend ache to your core?

Losing someone you love alters your life forever. You won't get over it, because they were the person you loved most dearly. They were your best friend. The pain may decrease over time, and new people may come into your life, but the gap never closes. How can you narrow the divide? Bridging it seems like an impossible task.

Losing someone who mattered enough to grieve over is not erased by anyone but death. This hole in the heart is in the shape of that person and no one else will ever fit, no matter how hard you try. Why would you want them to? You loved them more than anything else in this world and there is nothing you would like better than to hold on to them forever. But you also know deep down inside it's not for the best.

So, no matter how much your heart is going to break, you've got to let them go so they can know just how much you love them. So, they can be happy. If you're lucky, they'll come back, but if they do not, you can make it through. When your friend flies away and you know they will never come back, your tears may flow for a while. But one day, those tears will be tears of joy as happiness will reside in that broken heart of yours.

13. PURSUIT OF HAPPINESS

*"With unimaginable love also comes the
risk of unfathomable pain. And the deepest
souls hold out for such peril."*

JONATHON MUNCY STORM

Love is a powerful thing. It can lead to joy for some and sorrow for others. It comes with risks and rewards. It can give you pleasure and pain. Some souls will do anything to be loved, not just by anyone but in pursuit of their soulmate. Such uncertainties can lead to incomprehensible pain because you give everything you have and, in the end, you lose it all.

Love cannot be fully explored or understood. It cannot be measured, and its power is unrelenting. Love cannot be comprehended when it is far greater than your own. You can't fight fate, but you can control the love you spread to the world. When you know the attachment of love is intertwined with a perilous journey, only then will your appreciation become stronger and your devotion for the Lord more powerful.

When we encounter love, the risk, the threat, the uncertainty attached is only reserved for the dear souls who we believe deserve every minute and second of our time. Even if they are not meant to be in our life, we sacrifice our juncture for the mere opportunity to spend our time with them. The world is indeed full of peril, and in it there are many dark places; but still there is beauty in it, and though love mingles with grief, it grows stronger knowing it is life's greatest pursuit of happiness.

14. FIRE AND ICE

> *"There are two sides of me; one who loves you and another who hates you."*
>
> UNKNOWN

Fire and ice are a symbol of desire and hatred. They convey the idea that unchecked emotions can lead to destruction but also uncertainty. You can truly love someone and hate them at the same time. At one point, your love can exceed your dislike and at another moment, your hatred can exceed your passion. It is for this reason that you will feel like you are in different stages at the same time.

Have you ever felt that your heart was in two places? On its most vulnerable side, it adored them. It couldn't beat without them. Their love would always cause it to skip a beat. On its most tense side, it wanted to be left alone. It would detest them when they were moody and avoid them when they were not kind.

Their love destroyed you and left you with no words. Their adoration left a void, and you now have no self-confidence. Your dreams were shattered, and you lost the meaning of love. Every time you drew a story in your mind and painted your life on the walls, you found yourself undoing it all. They held your heart in one hand but seemed to forget about its presence in another. Your love couldn't fill the void of attention and care that they felt. If you are not worthy of love, are you worthy of hatred?

And when they left, you imagined the side that loves them was sobbing, and the side that hates them was celebrating. The day of their absence, joy met sadness inside you, like the meeting of fire and ice, destroying one another and you in the process.

15. SEPARATION

"And ever has it been known that love knows not its own depth until the hour of separation."

KHALIL GIBRAN

Love is limitless. You won't know how much you truly love someone until they are gone. Some leave us by walking away; others depart by death. Some distance themselves for a while and return. You can love someone all you want, but until they are separated from you, you will not fathom your true feelings for them.

Remember, there is a unique bond between you, and that love will always be there, not just in you but in them as well. That new person you thought replaced you, in fact, did not. You can't be replaced; there will always be only one you. They might try to replicate what you two had, but there is only one original Starry Night and you'll always be the masterpiece foolishly left behind.

If you love someone, tell them. Show them. Express what they mean to you. Walk them into love. Do not wait for tomorrow. Love them until you no longer can. Love them with all your heart before it's too late, because when that hour approaches, only then will you understand the profundity of infatuation.

16. BRAVERY

"The bravest thing you will ever do is love again."

MADALYN BECK

You both did the math. They added it all up and knew they had to let you go. You added it up and knew you had lost them. You could never prove your real worth, your real intentions. You couldn't change their mind. You thought you would die alone; That you would get sick or injured. The only thing you had control over was how and where it would happen. Or maybe you had no other options?

So, you imagined that you didn't want to be without them. You didn't want to be alone anymore. You wanted to go into a permanent sleep, but you couldn't even do that. Your longing for them was too much. You had power over nothing.

And that's when this feeling came over you like a warm blanket. You knew you had to somehow stay alive. You had to keep breathing, even though there was no reason to hope. Logic said you would never see them again, but you decided to stay alive and keep breathing.

One day, your logic was proven wrong because the tide came in and gave you a sail. To your surprise, they had come back to you. They returned. You were full of joy, but your happiness turned into tears once again. And then you realized you had lost them all over again. You were so sad that you didn't have them, but so grateful they were with you during that short period. You know you must keep breathing because tomorrow the sun will rise.

You always knew they were alive. You sensed it, but everyone in your circle said you had to stop loving them. That you had to let them go and move on. But how could you? They were the love of your life, and just maybe you would catch a glimpse of them before the sun sets. And when it does, you hoped that your memories of them would never fade. They will always live in your heart. Losing them once was devastating, but losing them a second time was heartbreaking. You will never get over this grief, but you must keep moving. It's the only way to withstand the power of love.

17. UNREQUITED LOVE

"The love that lasts the longest is the love that is never returned."

WILLIAM SOMERSETT MAUGHAM

Unrequited love is forbidden by its very nature. We mistake it for curiosity and longing for something as a necessity. This might be the most powerful and longest-lasting love because we will never attain it and hence never know what it is like. We will have no chance to be disappointed by this unreciprocated love because it is constantly raising our expectations through its prohibited essence.

Sometimes we don't get what we want. This heartbreak tends to last a lifetime. Even when we move on, it will always remain in our hearts. We will always yearn for what we want. In doing so, we come to grips with reality and question our existence. It is true that the love we never receive will last forever. We will always imagine what it would've been like. We anxiously want to know where it would lead us. We grapple with the mere thought of having the opportunity to have met them.

Waiting and hoping runs its course and we find ourselves in a dream that goes on and on. Over time, these emotions become stronger and precious to us. We hold on to them. Like music, they remain in our minds, and nothing can take them away from us. And that beautiful melody remains in our hearts forever.

18. CHOICES

> *"There's a reason I said I'd rather be alone. It wasn't because I thought I'd be happy alone. It was because I thought if I loved and then it fell apart, I might not make it."*

GREY'S ANATOMY

Having someone by your side is something we all aspire to. Having someone go through the same struggle in life is something most of us pursue. We seek attention and love when we are most vulnerable. Having the urge to be alone is sometimes not a matter of choice but of necessity. Some may call it selfishness; others may call it courage.

Truth is, we are raised differently. We have experienced life from different perspectives. We have faced unique challenges. We have developed from different backgrounds and family settings. These differences separate our thoughts, actions, and motivational aptitude. Each of us is unique. We see the world in a different shade of color, never identical to another person. We make choices, and sometimes they may be the wrong ones, but we learn and move forward.

The fear of failure can be daunting. It can limit our capabilities. It can blur our view of trust. Love is mysterious and comes with many traps and pitfalls, but it can also be the very thing that saves us from our insanity. Some seek love, knowing it can destroy them. Others avoid love, knowing they may lose the opportunity of a lifetime. If we shape our life around love and then it falls apart, the pain is too much. Losing love is like dying. The only difference is death ends. This can go on forever.

19. LOSS

"No one gives all of his heart twice, because the heart which was given once never comes back intact."

NIZAR QABBANI

It is true that the heart is fragile. When it breaks, it is never the same again. We can always love again, we can always move forward, but things will always be incomparable. The feeling and emotions will always be slightly different. Some of us pretend that things get better. Others make the best of their situation. Deep down inside, we know our hearts do not remain intact. The scars will always be there, reminding us of a time when we gave someone what was precious to us.

When you lose the love of your life, you lose a piece of yourself, the piece that holds you together. The piece that makes you the good person you've become; the piece that allows you to be you. So, when your heart gets broken, you get a break, in a sense. Heartbreak only really happens once in a lifetime. Once we experience such heartache, we are never the same again. We become different people, scarred and nerve damaged. We begin to look at life and love through a different shade of glass.

Love does so much damage because we allow ourselves to bask in that misery. We focus our attention on it and allow the painful thoughts and memories to fill our minds and seep into every aspect of our lives. We wait to be fixed while gradually becoming more and more broken.

20. COURAGE

> *"And as she walked away, I finally understood how sometimes the most courageous thing to do is to let another person love you."*

ROBERT M. DRAKE

It's courageous to allow someone to love you, but it's crucial to cultivate a strong sense of self-love too. You are worthy of love. You must recognize this so it can help you open yourself to receiving love.

It takes tenacity for a star to fall from the sky and into your hands. Then you allow it to seep through your veins and swim inside your blood and become every part of you. And then you must let it fly back into the sky. It's the most painful thing you'll ever have to do, and it won't be easy. But what's yours is yours. Whether it's up in the sky or in your hands. One day, it'll fall from the sky and hit you in the head. You will realize that allowing someone to love you was a good thing, perhaps even the best thing.

Maybe it was not meant to be, but a part of you will wish you had done more or allowed them closer to your heart.

Soulmates have a mutual destiny. There is a divine destiny to unite and fulfill our lives through a bond of love and friendship. Your meeting was the first of many miracles on your journey together. But destiny has limitations, and separation has its own unique evolutionary plan for your spiritual achievement. You must understand that you can never have what is not destined for you. You hope that you don't yearn and hold on to something that isn't yours, but you want your destiny to be with the one your heart desires.

Sometimes the plan to achieve a life together will not happen for many reasons unknown to us. Instead, there will be a growth in consciousness through fate. So, if you truly love someone, take the risk. Tell them how you feel. Show them you love them. Express what they mean to you. Walk them into love. Do not wait for tomorrow. Love them until you no longer can. Love them with all your heart before it's too late.

21. FATHER

"A father is neither an anchor to hold us
back, nor a sail to take us there, but a guiding
light whose love shows us the way."

UNKNOWN

A father is an incomparable soul, one who is always there to spill tears of happiness when his eyes fall upon his child. He is there with arms to catch them when they take their first steps. He is there to approve and disapprove, to accept and forgive. He is there to embrace his child and kiss them before they go to live and learn miles away.

A father is there to welcome his child home and let them hug him and smell the scent they remember from childhood. A father's warm, protective, comforting presence will always be missed during his absence. But most of all, he is always there to love his child, and they are always there to love him back. He is a daughter's first love. His love defines a love that only a daughter can comprehend. He is a son's first hero. His compassion leads to an understanding of what a true champion is.

There is a story behind every narrative. How you learned to ride a bicycle. How you got the courage to hike that mountain. How you learned to trust others. Sometimes the stories are easy, and sometimes they are difficult and tragic. But behind all your stories is always your father's story, because his is where yours begins. It's his love that will last you the rest of your life.

22. MOTHER

"There is absolutely no love in this world like the love of a mother. There is a void that cannot and will not ever be filled, no matter what anybody tells you."

JENNA ROSE

A mother is an irreplaceable soul, one who is there when heavy and sudden trials fall upon us. When adversity takes the place of prosperity, she will cling to us. When friends desert us, she will endeavor us by her kind precepts. When trouble thickens around us, she will counsel us to dissipate the clouds of darkness. Her presence will cause peace to return to our hearts.

A mother is the truest friend we will ever have. Her friendship leads to an understanding of what true companionship is. Her loss will devastate you. Her passing will transform you. Her absence will scar you for life. Such pain and the harrowing reality of not having your mother by your side can truly be painful.

There's a story behind every tale. How you learned to cook. How you excelled in school. How you developed the ability to love. Occasionally the tales are simple, and sometimes they are sad and heartbreaking. But behind all your stories is always your mother's story, because hers is where yours will eventually end. It's her affection that will complete your understanding of love for the rest of your existence.

23. LUMINESCENCE

"To me, love is about being able to see light inside of a person who sees nothing but darkness."

CAPED CRUSADER

There is not a single person who will avoid struggles and hardships in life. In fact, things that happen in life often shake us to our very core. The essential nature of being alive and being human is to experience life in its purest form, the wins and losses, celebrations and challenges, and the good with the bad. What we don't realize is that these struggles are a gift from life itself. When we come face to face with a struggle, a low point in life, be it an illness, a relationship breakdown or financial ruin, at the time we are lost in darkness.

Is there a person in your life who saw a way out of it? They understood you when seemingly no one else could. They could fathom your dark thoughts, the ones you weren't proud of, the ones that kept you up at night. Their soul could see the light in your darkness. It was in this place that their soul spoke to yours. They helped you realize that you were not your circumstances but something far greater.

The one person who comprehends you will ask you to go deeper into yourself and find the gold of who you are. Through darkness comes light, through fear comes love, and through pain comes triumph. This is the triumph of the human spirit. It is not in a select few; it is in every one of us.

In life, you can assume the victim role and feel sorry for yourself, or you can reach into the essence of who you are and find your inner strength. The one person who loves you will make you believe in yourself. Because you are powerful. You are amazing. If you are lucky enough to have this one person in your life, do everything in your power to hold on to them.

This book wants to see the light inside of you, when you see nothing but darkness in yourself. This text also believes in you. Its words are attempting to reach out to you to shine a beacon of hope through your shadow. The world needs your voice, your message, and your experiences so they can resonate in the hearts of others and give hope and courage to show that it is possible to overcome anything.

24. THE AWAKENING

"Love never dies; it just sleeps in your heart."

DARK NIGHT BEACON

Losing someone you love can be an incredibly difficult period of your life. After priceless moments spent with your companion, after sharing your time, your heart, and your life with your best friend, taking separate roads cannot be more heartbreaking. Love never dies. It doesn't know how to. It can get tired and feel pain, but love always wants to go for a walk. The heart might get one step before its aging tendons collapse into a heap on the floor, but that's what love does.

It's not that the heart dislikes company. On the contrary, a hike with you is all there is. That's what makes their world perfect, and in a perfect world, death and separation will always have a place. When you think love has died, know that it has just fallen asleep in your heart. Who would not cry? Love will thank you for a warm place to sleep and remain next to your heart, the best place there is.

When love first falls asleep, they wake up all the time, and that's why, of course, you cry all the time. So, you take a walk. It's a day full of adventure. Then you come home and it's night, and before you know it, a week and a month passes by. The love that you had was good, and you both know it. But it gets tiring being good; perhaps something was missing. Maybe love needed to rest. Maybe the two of you needed a break. So, understand this: after love has been sleeping in your heart, it will sleep longer.

But don't be fooled. Love is not dead. It is sleeping in your heart, and it will wake up, usually when you're not expecting it. Maybe it will wake up with endearment toward the same person. Perhaps it will start over. I feel sorry for people who don't have love sleeping in their heart. They miss the purpose of life. Its mysteries will always have a profound meaning and guide us through our journey. After all, it is this feeling and power that makes us human.

25. PAINTING

"Today I miss you a little more than yesterday."

GEMMA TROY

Sometimes feelings of deep longing for someone who is no longer in your life creeps up when you least expect it. A certain song comes. Maybe you travel to places that remind you of them. Or you're home alone and can't help but reminisce about all the fun times the two of you had together.

It started out as simply picking up a paintbrush and painting on a blank canvas, but the reality was different. You were painstakingly passing the time and distracting yourself from the overwhelming feelings of loneliness that gripped you. Your mind and body ached to feel their touch, to hear their voice and their thoughts, to have a conversation. You craved their presence in any form. It's strange how missing someone feels. You're not lonely, necessarily, but rather you want that person so much that everyone and everything else seems irrelevant.

You long for that smile, that kiss, and those words, and it's as though nothing else on Earth can satisfy. You can only distract yourself until you're able to be blessed again. This is a dangerous place to be. When the act of missing someone starts to consume you, when it starts to immobilize your mind and turns you into a non-functioning human being who can't focus on anything else, this is a sure sign you're growing attached. There's a lot of emphasis on the negative aspects of missing someone, but this is only because the attached way of loving someone has become the human default.

When you're really missing someone, take a moment to be grateful that you're missing someone at all. This is an amazing connection to have with another human being, so embrace these feelings. Accept them and maybe even allow it to make you smile as you paint your love story to your heart's content.

26. LASTING EFFECT

"Once you have read a book you care about,
some part of it is always with you."

LOUIS L. AMOUR

It's true that love sticks. The books we read will end, but the feelings that come with them often follow us. I've been there, so much so that I never stopped caring for some of the stories and characters I've stumbled across while reading.

I don't know if this is because true love is stubborn, or whether I am simply stubborn when I love a book.

But even when that book deeply harms me, it's difficult to let it go. Maybe that's why I keep reading books that break my heart, even when it's clear the book will have an ending of some sort. Is this something I am doing to myself, or is it that true love never dies?

True love might never die completely, but it experiences reincarnation. The love I experience in a book goes through many cycles. When I allow love to be a force that transforms me, I experience many cycles, too. I read a book, fall in love, and even if the book doesn't meet my standards, I can be certain that I will see that love again. It might not look the same the second time around, but the love I feel will be even stronger than it was before.

Have you wept bitter tears because a wonderful story came to an end? When you must take your leave of the characters with whom you have shared so many adventures, whom you have loved and admired. I reach a point where my hopes and fears grow with the characters, and life seems empty and meaningless without their company. Have you ever felt a deep level of understanding from the books you read? If such things have not been part of your experience, you probably won't understand the miracle of reading.

27. SOMEBODY ELSE

*"I don't want your body, but I hate to think
about you with somebody else."*

THE 1975

There are people who don't want to be with someone, but they also don't want that person to be with someone else. It's selfish to think somebody might not want to be with somebody anymore, but they still don't want to see them with somebody else. Maybe it's because they were wronged or failed their expectations, but the thought of them being with someone else kills them inside. The thought of them connecting with someone is devastating. When they break up with someone, their feelings may fade. They don't want to get back with them, but seeing them move on still hurts, because they promised forever. Getting over someone is difficult, and they may feel irrelevant.

Jealousy is one of the reasons it's hard for us to let go. We may regret past decisions and not want the other to move on. We may even try to get back with them. But it doesn't always work. They fell deeply in love with them, but both of them struggled in the relationship and it ended. Now they must get over the lost love of their life.

They became too intoxicated to know what was happening or what was going on. They weren't good enough, and that's why their love left them. They realized this and talked about how they missed them, wishing them good luck in their new beginning. They became depressed about the breakup, and they tried to move on. They began to hallucinate encounters to help deal with the pain and the guilt they were feeling from the separation. They didn't like thinking about it, but they were experiencing guilty jealousy. They didn't want the person back, but they certainly didn't want someone else to have them either.

28. HEART ROCK

*"Love is a cliff, a clear, cold curve of stone, mottled by
stars, smirched by the morning, carved by the dark
sea. Till stars and dawn and waves can slash no more.
Till the rock's heart is found and shaped again."*

JAMES WRIGHT

Like love, finding heart rocks sometimes happens when
I'm not deliberately looking for them. Do you find yourself stumbling upon heart-shaped boulders when you are
simply hiking in nature? It's like meditation, not thinking and opening your senses to the smell of the sea, the
growling of the surf, and the shapes of rocks. In those
moments, the heart rock will appear, as if that stone has
waited millennia for me to discover it.

The universe works with nature to mold rocks into
any shape it desires. Each of these rocks is formed
by physical changes, such as melting, cooling, eroding, compacting, or deforming. Sedimentary rocks are
formed from pieces of other existing rock or organic
material. Like the transformation of a rock, love also
requires time and revision. It requires patience, sacrifice,
and attention. There will be etches of struggle and signs
of appreciation, and these imperfections will develop
and be recognized as true love.

Maybe the cosmos is giving me a hint. Perhaps the
universe is providing me with a sign. In the vast depths
of creation, maybe I'm being told to spread love. To share
my heart with someone, to lend a hand to a friend, to
aid someone in need. The beautiful heart rock appears
right before me and empowers me to forgive others and

let go of the past, to ensure my heart doesn't become as hard as that rock. Someone may have hurt me, but not everyone will. Yes, I will be vulnerable, but I must trust again. My Lord wants me to continue my journey, having faith in Him and His creations.

29. SACREDNESS

"There is a place where someone loves you both before and after they learn who you are."

NEIL HILBORN

Is it possible to love someone you have never met? A person who has yet to learn about you and whose path has never crossed yours. There is something inside your soul waiting for their presence, but it is an utter mystery to you until you meet them. You may have a mysterious connection with that person, yet neither of you know the other exists.

Soulmates are typically thought of as souls our quintessence knows. If the basic model of human being is an embodiment cloaked in form, then a soulmate could absolutely be someone you have never met. Love coexists between scattered parts of souls that have become divided in this physical universe, a union affected within the substance of their original sublime element. The harmony of their love in the divine world is their everlasting home. The principles of their attraction are established long before they ever meet.

Loving someone before and after you truly learn who they are taps into the complexity of love—the contrast between idealized infatuation and the reality of knowing someone fully, flaws and all. Love can evolve or fracture in the face of revelation, testing the strength of the bond between two people.

Learning who someone really is can shatter illusions. Can you still love someone once you know their full reality? Loving someone after learning who they are means accepting their flaws, complexities, and contradictions. Will you decide to stay after seeing someone's imperfections?

There is a venue where love exists when loving someone else is unthinkable. There is a residence where your heart does not want anyone else but them. In that place, you find yourself with the thoughts and memories of a once-upon-a-love-story that had a beautiful beginning and a sorrowful ending.

30. THE MINUTE

"Years of love have been forgot, in the hatred of a minute."

EDGAR ALLEN POE

Pain and sorrow caused by a brief moment of hatred or conflict can overshadow and outweigh years of love and happiness. Negative experiences can have a disproportionately strong impact on our emotions and memories compared to positive ones.

What if hatred can destroy someone's spirit, that immaterial part of them that God treasures? Is it possible to mangle someone's soul with hatred? Is it possible to wound their heart? Is it possible, if someone is mean or abusive enough, that they can emotionally wound someone beyond repair?

In this world of fear, uncertainty, and constant change, hatred seems to permeate our every day. The daily news is filled with uncontrolled actions of hate, of vitriol spewing from the mouths of so many, of emotions out of control, propelled by hate to quickly pierce the soul of everyone in range. How do you overcome hate with love in a hate-filled world?

Intense love can quickly turn to intense hatred. Even years of shared love and closeness between two people can be quickly forgotten or discarded in the face of a sudden strong negative emotion like hatred. It speaks to the fragility of human relationships and how quickly they can break down, even after a long history.

Unexpectedly positive emotions can quickly give way to their opposites. What a sense of profound loss and disappointment when love is destroyed in such a fashion. The destructive power of hate can erode or obliterate the forces of healing connection by resentment, anger or betrayal. Like growth and decay, hatred can consume the positive symbol of love, turning what was once beautiful into something bleak.

It's important to nurture and maintain relationships, even when faced with challenges. Letting hatred or other negative emotions take over can undo a lifetime of shared experiences and affection. The fragility of the human heart and the constant vigilance required to preserve our most meaningful connections is at stake and can all be taken away in a minute.

CHAPTER V

DESTINY

Our deeds determine our fate. We have the power to shape our own destiny through our thoughts and actions. Self-reliance, empowerment, and the belief that we can control our journeys through our own efforts and choices is critical to self-growth. In this chapter, you will transform into seeing the good things that happen in your life as miracles and the unfortunate moments as divine. The day you know what you want is the day your past and future come together in clarity. Predestination never takes away from your free will, and if you want to delve into the truth, you must seek your Creator to obtain your inherent possibilities and self-direction.

1. THE BEGINNING

> *"Never give up. There is no such thing as an ending, just a new beginning."*

UNKNOWN

The beacon in my dark night encourages me when I feel unworthy that I should appreciate change. When I feel down, I find myself reading inspirational quotes to know I am not alone in my suffering and that there is hope.

The mindset of a new beginning involves embracing change, optimism, and growth. It may not be easy, but developing a mindset that embraces resilience, and a sense of possibility will give you the path to hope and a newfound meaning in life. Always remember that you are destined for greatness, and when your mindset is wrapped around this positive thinking, you are capable of great adventures.

There's no such thing as a completely fresh start. Everything new arrives on the heels of something old, and every beginning comes at the cost of an ending. The secret to a good life is to pay more attention to the beginnings than the endings. So many people say they want a new life, but then they take the new one for granted. Don't do this to yourself. Don't hold on to what's no longer there. Don't wait until your life is almost over to realize how priceless the present moment is. The good life is here. It begins right now, when you stop wanting a different one.

2. THE REPRISAL

"I will have my vengeance, in this life or the next."

MAXIMUS DECIMUS MERIDIUS

Was that traumatic incident part of some higher order that orchestrated the creation of who I am today? I may never know the answer to that question. Perhaps it was merely by chance or luck. Some might call it fate, others a calling or simply a mission. But when I look closer, there is a definite purpose to my life, making sense of the chaos it has become. This idea is at the heart of many, if not all, religions. The belief that nothing happens without God's will and that His will supersedes all human will.

I went through a life-changing experience, one that bruised me to my core and tested my limits of faith and patience. Only strong individuals will understand the pain and seek patience. There is no greater agony and suffering than enduring a disturbing encounter, but the promise of vengeance is guaranteed by God. Have you ever been wronged? Have you felt betrayed? Did someone ruin something that was precious to you? We have all been taken advantage of at some point, and there is nothing more we want than to seek revenge.

Perhaps you lost a loved one. Maybe you were cheated on or lied to. Maybe you were the victim of trauma. In any situation where we feel betrayed, it is normal to feel anger. We immediately want justice. Our hearts want payback for what was done. We believe we will become whole once the other person receives their karma.

Your Lord sees all. Nothing transpires without His knowledge. And when evil is done, there will be a price to pay. Perhaps the consequences will be delayed for the here-after, but no action will be unanswered. And when you realize that nothing is in your hands, you will understand the power of God and the true meaning of vengeance.

3. THE BEACH

*"I suppose I thought if I sat very still,
the world wouldn't move."*

JOHN PATRICK

I thought if I stood still, maybe the world would come to a halt. That maybe, if I stared at the ocean, calm would take over. Because at the beach, life is different. Time doesn't move by the hour but by the moment. We are at the mercy of the currents, attentive to the tides and followers of the moon.

I've always found the sea an excellent form of visual meditation. It's one of the few things that gets more inter-esting the longer you stare at it. Waves jostle and hiss on the sand. Unidentified bird calls give the whole thing a nice nautical feel. Do you ever wonder where the waves go? Do you ever contemplate how the ripples flows? Do you ever think about the depth of the ocean? Do you ever admire how the humble water molecule is responsible for all living things? Our destiny is tied to what our hearts desire.

The beach is where I find peace. No other place can provide the serene sounds, the natural breeze, and the jaw dropping flow of water. It's where dreams are made, songs are written, stories are told. It's where ideas are created, love is born, and peace is found. Feelings of calm and peace surround me and staring at the ocean puts me into a mild meditative state. The consistent ebbing and flowing of sound, coupled with the visuals, allows me to relax and feel more engaged. The smell of the ocean breeze contributes to a soothing state, and the touch of the sand makes me feel alive.

The beach can sometimes be lonely and unpredictable. It can sometimes be inspiring. Every day is different. Every moment is special. You must be aware and open your senses; smell the sea, feel the sun, taste the salt, and life becomes an adventure. Your destiny is a divine secret that is predetermined by your Lord. Along with death and sustenance, God never takes your volition, and the outcome of those choices is governed only by His will.

4. LIFE

"What is the meaning of life? One that tended to close in on one with years, the great revelation had never come. Instead, there were little daily miracles, illuminations, matches struck unexpectedly in the dark; here was one."

VIRGINIA WOOLF

Your life can be fulfilled when you reach your spiritual peak and are in divine communion with God. Is this your goal and foundation in life? Year after year, I looked for the answer. I searched for the unmasking of my soul. I uncovered an elusive truth that haunted me for most of my life.

Your Lord encourages you to present yourself before Him in the utmost humility and to desperately seek His

Mercy in order to create an intimate bond. Use your birthday as a day of reflection and gratitude. The day your story began was prophesied. Your intentions and journey in life were written. How you choose to go about the trek is ultimately in your hands.

In the dark night, I waited in silence for a beacon of hope. As my memories and experiences ran wildly in my mind, I couldn't help but remember my childhood, all those moments I was too naive to understand. Little did I know that daily revelations were indeed upon me; I just had to ponder deeply about my destiny before I could understand it.

Finding gratitude in challenging times can be incredibly powerful. Every struggle you face builds your resilience and brings you closer to your Creator. As another birthday passes me by, I am thankful for another blessed night. Take time to celebrate your uniqueness and the qualities that make you who you are. By focusing on these aspects, you can fully embrace and appreciate the milestone of another birthday. May peace be upon your next day of birth.

5. THE COSMOS

"You are the clear book, through whose letters; All that is secret is revealed and made known."

IMAM ALI

You may feel unimportant, but your soul is a part of our vast universe. You may think you are unnoticed, but your being permeates all things in the cosmos. You are destined to advance toward the place where you are invited for eternal bliss. It is written for you to turn your face away from the vicious world.

God sometimes gives us moments of perfect peace. In this period, we love and believe that we are loved; in this instant, we have formulated our creed wherein all is clear and holy to us. Grace is within us. Grace *is* us. It is not something to be acquired from others. If it is external, it is useless. It is only necessary to know its existence is in you. You are never out of its operation. We are a self-organizing system that learns to adapt, just like our universe. We are conscious beings who came from the eternal energy of the universe. All the secrets we seek are within us.

During a star gazing trip high atop the hills of Death Valley, I contemplated the secrets we desire to know but aren't prepared to understand. The shooting stars were a sign of the letters we seek, our own DNA, the building blocks of life. The night sky has captivated the human imagination for centuries, inspiring aw and wonder. The celestial wonders can symbolize a promise between God and His believers, offering reassurance in times of doubt.

Remember that you are the universe. Some part of your being knows this is where you came from. You long to return. Go out and gaze at the night sky. The fleeting stars you observe are your symbol of spiritual awakening, prompting you to reflect on your faith and purpose. And you will return one day, stronger than ever, because the cosmos is also within you.

6. EXISTENCE

"Try to make sense of what you see and wonder about what makes the universe exist."

STEPHEN HAWKING

Why does the universe exist? This is a cosmic mystery. Why is there a world, why are we in it, and why is there something rather than nothing at all? The philosopher, Arthur Schopenhauer said that "those who don't wonder about the contingency of their existence, of the contingency of the world's existence, are mentally deficient."

God created the whole universe and made it subservient to mankind so they could explore and harness nature. Harnessing and pondering over phenomena in nature is a moral obligation and a part of the humans' trusteeship on earth. People who have the right knowledge and sincerity to study carefully and objectively are more cognizant of God's power and mercy and are more God-fearing than those who are ignorant.

The universe is drifting toward disorder. The question of how it became so remarkably ordered in the first place also points to God. If you see a rock on a mountain, you wouldn't know how it got there. If you see a watch there, you will know it has a designer because of the complexity and order of the watch. Similarly, we can know God exists from the order and complexity of the universe.

Human beings have an inward sense of morality. This presupposes an absolute value and standard to which we make comparisons, and this is God. This is how we apply natural law, and these values of right and wrong were written upon the hearts of humans so that those who knew not the law were able to abide by the law. The one who wrote this knowledge of right and wrong on the hearts of mankind is God. Remember to look up at the stars and not down at your feet. Be curious. And however difficult life may seem, there is always something you can do and succeed at. Don't give up. You are destined for success!

7. KNOWLEDGE

"When you already know that the answer will hurt you, respect your heart and don't ask."

ARABIC QUOTE

There will come a time when you know the answer. It will be revealed to you, written in your heart. An answer that you have been patiently waiting for, but not the one you wanted. The explanation will hurt you. It will make you cry. It will pain you to your core. The answer will not be easily understood. The resolution will make you think. In life, not everything is meant to be understood. Not all things are meant to be comprehended. You will question your existence.

Sometimes destiny is not on our side. Sometimes it has other plans. You must accept your fate and believe that everything happens for a reason. It is not about being selfish; it is about knowing the inevitable. You are doing exactly what you should be doing. Either you are being tested by God or He is attempting to bring you closer to Him. If you walk toward your Lord, He will come running to you. Always stay positive. The number of blessings your Creator gives you far outweighs your sins.

Happiness is difficult to achieve. Your heart has a connection with your Lord. Remember that the next time you ponder why your destiny has been unhappy. Keep your heart clean of evil and permanently place the remembrance of God, for He will remember you. Put your hand over your heart. Think of that hand pressed close to your body. Feel your heart beating to the tune of your Lord. The heart is that spiritual part of us where our emotions and desires dwell. It is also where your answers come from.

When that time comes, don't ask. Your heart already knows. Respect it. Give it the benefit of the doubt. Your heart knows you, feels you, and understands you. The heart grasps what we cannot understand. In the end, it is your heart that will forever be with you. Take good care of it and it will take care of you.

8. THE EGO

"When you allow your ego to control your thoughts, everything you believe becomes an illusion."

RUSTY ERIC

They didn't believe me when I told them the truth. They refused to listen when I tried to explain. Doubt clouded their mind. Their perception was drowned by their lack of understanding. They never gave themselves a chance to hear me, didn't give themselves the opportunity to know the truth. They find themselves in a cast of lies manifesting from their uncertainty. Like an illusion, they cheated themselves from righteousness.

Their hesitation may have seemed harmless, but they lost more than a person. They unfairly deprived themselves of being with the one. They failed to comprehend my kind heart, instead allowing themselves to be surrounded by confusion. Their minds were set, and they lost a good soul. Finding someone as dear as me will not be easy; not everyone is created to carry the burden of removing a strong ego. And with every passing day, they quietly wonder and secretly regret losing the one who cared for them the most.

Your fate is tied to your ego, and it is proportionate to your success and intelligence. If your sense of self becomes clouded, your life can become a mirage. When we fail to realize the magnitude of our decisions, we lose a part of us. When we allow falsehood in our lives, we allow it to conquer our beliefs. When we engage in wrongfulness, we carry the burdens of those who seek evil. And sadly, we lose our loved ones because the ego has conquered our heart.

The ego can be both a guide and an obstacle in the journey towards one's destiny, depending on how it is managed and transcended. Only when you are free from distractions and self-centered motivations, will you recognize your higher calling and authentic self. It is through the lens of ego which we interpret and pursue what we consider to be our destiny.

9. DEPENDENCY

> *"Don't depend too much on anyone in this world because even your own shadow leaves you when you are in darkness."*

IBN TAYMIYYAH

Depending too much on someone else has consequences. When you rely solely on someone else, you place yourself at risk. You become blind to your surroundings. The darkness will consume you, and even your shadow will leave you. This is one of the consequences when you place too much trust in someone else.

If you depend too much on someone else, you will ultimately be disappointed. They will, in fact, leave you. It's hard to believe that life has such places of darkness that everyone will disappear. It is difficult to understand that you will eventually be alone.

Not relying on others too much can lead to a deeper sense of independence and resilience. You can nurture internally, by being more confident in your decision-making and abilities. Focus on your own journey, knowing that your path is unique, and your pace is your own.

People leave us in many ways. People pass away and we must mourn their deaths. People break up from relationships and we must cope with their absence. People move out of their homes and relocate to another area, and we must find a way to replace their tenure. People may endure long-term illness or injury, and we must accept their situation until they heal. Losses can be permanent or temporary. To trust in others to the extent that you have no provision for yourself is a recipe for disaster. The above quote doesn't say don't depend on anyone; it simply says don't depend *too much* on somebody else. We come into this world alone and we depart from it alone.

10. RISK

"Only those who will risk going too far can possibly find out how far one can go."

THOMAS STEARNS ELIOT

Life is measured by the number of moments that take our breath away. That's the reason why I hope to see things that amaze me. I hope to feel things I can dream about. I hope to live a life my loved ones can be proud of. If I find that I'm not, I hope to have faith to begin a spiritual journey seeking the truth. To find the truth and the limits of my ability, I must go to the edge.

But how and where do we find this edge? We must push past challenges and beyond our personal limits. When life feels like we're standing at the edge, unsure of what's next, remember that the most profound growth happens just outside our comfort zone. We truly transform when we dare to face uncertainty, embrace discomfort and push through fear. Keep reminding yourself: You are stronger than you think, and the edge is not your limit, it's your launchpad.

People will claim they can't do something when it is merely outside their comfort zone, rather than truly being beyond how far they can go. By testing ourselves, by pushing our limits and trying again, we get better. We find new things to try, new methods or tactics, and eventually we get better. By pushing the limits, we learn what we excel at, what we are good at, and where we need improvement. And if we have not accomplished our goal yet because we couldn't get the pieces to fit, perhaps we need to go back over our mistakes and learn from our experiences.

By risking failure, by pushing beyond your abilities, you will find your ceiling. Once you know your limitations, you can either accept them or work on improving yourself. Failure is never the answer. The correct answer will depend on the value you place on improvement. One day, you will realize how far you have come and how your fate was tied to your fortitude and willingness to push your capabilities to the limit.

11. GENEROSITY

"Always gracefully let go of things not meant for you because an open heart will always be rewarded by the generosity that it creates."

BUDDHA

Life has many setbacks and often we can be humbled by those challenges. Things that once seemed perfect no longer fit into our lives, and the goals we once dreamed of accomplishing have been replaced by new ones. We find ourselves challenged by what we were raised to believe, enlightened by the new people we meet, and immersed in the new environment around us. Suddenly, we find ourselves completely changed.

It's hard to admit when we've grown apart from someone, especially if that person once fit perfectly into our lives. This person could be anyone—a friend, a family member, or even a past love. We shouldn't feel guilty about letting someone go who was once so important to us. People change. It's important to value the memories we shared but be unafraid to stand alone. We can be our own priority.

Deep down, I know I'll never be the same. Losing that special someone was unexpected and unforeseen. Just as I was starting to get life figured out, things came crashing down around me. But then I realized something spectacular—that maybe this is part of the journey. Maybe I haven't fully accepted this yet. It is a scary reality to face, but it is an important part of the journey.

Somewhere along the way, however, I discovered that some dreams are unattainable. Some souls are not meant to be kept, and it's difficult to let them go. It's difficult to be told you're not good enough, especially when it's something you've wanted since you were young. Fight for your dreams and future, but be wise enough to realize and accept if something is not meant for you.

12. THE UNBREAKABLE

"Someday someone will break you so badly that you'll become unbreakable."

JOKER

At some point in your life, someone will hurt you. You will be let down; you will be disappointed. Your heart will ache. There will come a time when you reach the lowest low. You will be unable to think clearly, and you will feel like you've lost a part of yourself. You will know what it is to be damaged.

For me, life lost all meaning during a phase of my existence. Something hurt me to the point that everything was tainted. I could not trust anyone, and everyone was assumed to be evil. Once this occurred, nothing had value anymore because everything could be taken or corrupted. My response was to protect myself from more pain by emotionally detaching from everyone and everything. Nothing could hurt me because nothing mattered. I was not free of pain; rather, I built walls and isolated myself to the point that it was easier to not speak and hope the world forgot me.

Anger and rage died because nothing was worth being angry over. This robbed me of the ability to enjoy anything. It was easier to pass on anything potentially enjoyable because it could also turn painful. Love, hope, loyalty, trust, and friendship became lies, even hateful.

To be broken is emptiness itself. This can be a difficult challenge to overcome. I felt trapped by the negative thoughts that circled constantly in my mind. Part of the blame was placed on some sort of mental health factor, and the rest on myself for being such a failure. Sadly, these dark thoughts never seemed to go away.

There are two things that may happen to a broken person. First, they become so soft that no one and nothing can break them physically. Secondly, they become so hard that nothing and no one can break them mentally. Is this your current reality? If so, what are you doing to change it? Forgiveness is the beginning of the healing process, even if it's only for your own peace of mind. The journey from brokenness to wholeness is often non-linear and full of setbacks. Every small effort you make to rise after loss can contribute to a stronger, more resilient version of yourself. Call upon your Lord to help you, and that broken soul of yours shall soon be at peace.

13. THE SEARCH

"I know where I'm going and I know the truth, and I don't have to be what you want me to be. I'm free to be what I want."

MUHAMMAD ALI

You won't always have a clear philosophy. Sometimes you won't live up to the principles you espoused, but never stop asking questions. Success is the only option when you stay positive. When you seek, you shall find the truth. No one will hand you rectitude. You must find it yourself. Do not accept truthfulness unless you find evidence to back up its claim. To know with certainty is to understand beyond a reasonable doubt.

Study and learn with an open mind. Seek veracity. Look for righteousness. Find goodness, morality, certitude, and probity. Stay away from falsehood. Seek shelter from deception and subterfuge. Avoid chicanery and treachery. Distance yourself from fabrications. Truth is always open and straightforward. It never hides anything and is unable to conceal what it wants. Truth has no fear and is full of patience. Its words are deep and meaningful, and its law is firm and just.

The truth has the soul of a flame. It has no partners, and its message is always clear. When the truth emerges and grips your attention, its shadows become your facts. The truth always wins because it's the image of God. You will gain an abundance of success in life when you utilize the power of truth, because the truth holds to last. Your destiny is tied to the hidden truth inside your heart.

Knowing the truth and becoming who you want to be is a journey of self-awareness and courage. The truth often holds a mirror to our deepest fears, insecurities, and limitations, but it also reveals our potential, strengths, and purpose. Once you confront the truth about yourself, your circumstances, or your dreams, you empower yourself to break free from illusions or doubts. Being who you want to be requires aligning your actions with your values and passions. It's not just about success but about authenticity. The most powerful transformation happens when you stop trying to fit into someone else's mold and start living in alignment with your own truth. This journey isn't always easy, but it's liberating. Believe in the power of honesty and perseverance. The truth gives you the clarity to overcome obstacles, and embracing your authentic self gives you the strength to live the life you truly want.

14. REALITY

"I can't go back to yesterday because I was a different person then."

LEWIS CARROLL

Life experiences, often painful ones, impact our lives and change us profoundly. It can be hard to let go of the past. We find ourselves wanting to go back in history to when things were better, more comfortable and familiar. But the past is the past. Life changes us. We must accept that. There is no point ruminating or indulging in the past, no reason to feel sorry for yourself about the trials and tribulations of yesterday. Looking backward won't move you forward in life; it will only lead to failure.

Change is inevitable. We cannot always anticipate it, but we can choose how we respond to it. Accept change for what it is and learn to embrace it. It is an opportunity for growth and allows us to transform. Every day, we get another chance, a blank paper for us to write the next chapter of the story of our lives, a blank canvas to paint our next journey. Success is in our hands, and we must decide how to change to signify our present.

I often remember yesterday with regret. The new and different person I have become is better than the person I once was. It is human nature to experience change and grow along the way. I must accept this new reality and cherish it. My goal is to become a different person than I was yesterday by growing stronger, smarter, and more unique. Like the universe, life won't stop moving and changing. Without change, the universe would not exist, and its survival depends on this movement.

The same is true of who you are. If you compare today with yesterday and find that nothing has changed, you haven't been living life to its fullest. Life gives us both good and bad experiences, but we choose how they define us. When you discover your potential, success awaits you. Your destiny is in front of you. Don't look back!

15. CHILDHOOD

*"When we are children, we seldom think of the future.
This innocence leaves us free to enjoy ourselves as
few adults can. The day we fret about the future
is the day we leave our childhood behind."*

PATRICK ROTHFUSS

When I was young, I was not the same as the other kids. It was okay to be uncanny, a little different from the others. I didn't feel like I belonged, but I was distinctly me. I came to realize that being different and thinking differently was my biggest strength. Despite what other people suggested, I did whatever I felt inclined to do. My free-spirited nature both entertained the people around me and drove them crazy. While some of their advice was worthwhile, I didn't know everything I thought I did. I didn't have to worry about growing up and the responsibilities that came with it.

As I grew older, I looked back at several risible things I did when I was young. I tried to figure out why I was allowed to be such a rascal. Then one day I realized that there was no harm done. They made for great stories. I love reading and writing more than anything else. After surviving the rollercoaster of trying to learn to write, I began to write to my heart's content. I began to read my favorite stories in a graceful manner, reading and picking quotes as I went along, then detailing those sayings to my heart's content.

I was never really stressed over school problems, my enemies, and those who pretended to be my friend. But some of it did hinder my success. In some moments, they seemed to be a distraction toward my goals and dreams. I recognized that school was a phase that everyone was trapped in until they moved on and made progress toward self-realization. That's when it dawned on me that I left my youth the moment I began to plan for my career.

The instant I realized that the opinions of others were not of importance to me, and I had full control of my destiny in life. My success was waiting for me. We should not try to win the approval of people who don't want us in their lives. We won't change that much when we're older. We'll be a little wiser and a little taller, but with the same innocent heart as a child.

16. FEAR

"It's good to be scared. It means you still have something to lose."

RICHARD WEBBER

It's okay to be afraid. Being scared means you're about to do something brave. It means you have worked toward whatever fear you may have, and you want to conquer the task at hand. Being afraid is not a sign of weakness. It means you are human. It means you are willing to risk something that matters to you. It means you understand its consequences. It's something important to you, so much so that you cannot fathom the chance of failure.

Your emotions may swing from terrified to awkward and uncomfortable. You will feel intolerable. Your limits will be tested. But it's all part of the journey that will make you stronger. Feeling vulnerable and exposed scares anyone, but have confidence in yourself. You will make it through.

I was scared when I experienced my trauma. I was alone, helpless, young, and vulnerable. But I knew deep down that I had to fight to survive. I had to restore my confidence. Knowing I could never undo the pain, I promised to have the courage to never again be in that situation.

After my life-changing experience, I often experienced intense fright. But slowly I built the determination to never to let myself be overcome by fear again. The next time you feel scared and worried to seize a moment, remember it's a good thing to be afraid, but don't allow it to blur your focus. Being afraid means you understand the risks, possibilities, and potential. Don't fear your destiny, for it is the sum of your past and present combined with your level of confidence and faith.

17. MAGIC

"Those who don't believe in magic will never find it."

ROALD DAHL

Do you believe in magic? We make our own magic by the way we think, the visions we dream, the goals we set, and our sight for our future. When we hope for great things, we believe that great things will come. When we set our sights on goals that seem bigger than we ever imagined, we set our course to be filled with magic and amazement.

Our attitude about our lives plays the greatest role in our level of happiness. Have you ever seen people with next to nothing material in their lives who are incredibly happy? Have you seen people who are facing difficult trials still see the magic that exists all around them? We choose to make magic in our lives. We choose to have hope and faith for good things to come. We choose to believe that every situation we face is meant to help us grow and improve and excel in our lives. We choose to let the magic happen.

When we see ourselves as lucky and blessed, we notice our surroundings much more. We look for positivity when we feel our lives are lucky. We notice people and opportunities in our paths because we are looking for those fortunate encounters to take place, and so they do.

As we head into the future, I hope you can believe in the magic that exists in your life because when you believe it, it comes true. Above all, watch the world around you with glittering eyes, because the greatest secrets are always hidden in the most unlikely places.

18. PATIENCE

"Be sure that there is something waiting for you after much patience, to astonish you to a degree that you forget the bitterness of the pain."

IMAM ALI

Patience is a characteristic of enlightenment that develops in the heart. It is a comprehensive virtue that encompasses perseverance, endurance, forbearance, diligence, and restraint. The virtue of patience is tremendously important for our well-being. We must strive to develop patience within ourselves. It is our destiny to understand our journey in life with great stoicism.

God has made patience like a lion that never gets tired, a soldier that can never be defeated, a castle that can never be breached. Patience and victory are of the same kind. Just as victory comes with patience, relief comes with distress, and ease comes with hardship. Forbearance is a core concept of many beliefs around the world and leads to peace by improving social relationships and self-improvement. God will bestow patience upon those who encourage improvisation and facilitate bricolage.

Restraint comes to those who wait. It helps without any need, and its relationship to victory is like that of the head to the body. Tolerance is an admirable quality that helps us connect to God. It speaks and acts upon the truth and endures through hardship. Fortitude does not teach us to remain silent, but neither does it encourage confrontation. Being patient is patience with the help of God. We persevere because the promise of the Lord is true, and our patience is tied to our destiny.

19. ENLIGHTENMENT

"At the center of your being, you have the answer; you know who you are, and you know what you want."

LAO TZU

How marvelous is it to know that at the center of your being, the center of your soul, you have the answer to that ultimate life question of who you are and what you want. The entirety of one's soul and the depths of its unique powers are unlimited. Each of us goes through our lives constantly asking, "Who am I?" and "What do I want?" We search for the answers, seeking them in an object, person, a goal, or a task. While that's not a bad thing, we won't find the answers to the questions at hand—or at least we are taking the longest, most convoluted road to them.

The key lies in our wisdom and life experiences. We have the answers already. Deep within us, we have a certain knowing that aches for enlightenment and attention. It is poised and ready to provide the guidance and solutions we seek, but we must turn inward to receive them. That can be difficult, especially in a world that holds so much credence outward.

It is not impossible, however, to circumvent our outward, peer-approval, and pressured society and listen instead to our inner guide. To seek out the answers that we know ring true for us, not anyone else. Some of us have walked both roads and have lost ourselves to outward pressures and false answers. To come home, back to yourself and your soul, is a blessing that will help you see just how wise and sure you can be.

Don't despair if you've fallen off-course or lost touch with your inner guide. They will always be there, waiting with endless patience for you to return to yourself, to return home. Don't fear the answers either, for they are yours. You are absolute and amazing. Who you are and what you want are reflections of that.

20. THE BRIDGE

"We build too many walls and not enough bridges."
SIR ISAAC NEWTON

What walls have you built to protect yourself? You may have found that they separate you from others to the point of disconnection, loneliness, and seclusion. Bridges, on the other hand, join and connect. Bridges help us come together as a community to create more than we can manage on our own. We tend to create walls in our minds. We create too many limitations, obstacles, and problems instead of creating solutions and finding ways to make things better.

Why do people create mental barriers? Because it doesn't take much effort. They produce a roadblock because they are afraid of change and see transformation as something negative. But change is an essential part of life, and it is a mistake to make it our enemy. Building walls creates the illusion of protection and safety but stalls and hinders our journey to success and growth.

We should be more open-minded and imaginative, think positively and look for ways to solve problems and make things better. We should not look for excuses or ways to avoid acting for the better. We must get out of our comfort zone and allow what is destined for us, even if it means change is necessary. Being unbiased is a virtue that allows people to consider multiple perspectives, tolerate different viewpoints, and learn from others. Most importantly, as a believer, being unprejudiced allows you to seek knowledge, which becomes a sign of strength and provides you with the ability to better understand your own faith.

21. FRIENDSHIP

"The realest people don't have a lot of friends."

TUPAC SHAKUR

If you have a small circle of friends, be proud. If your connections are limited, be humble. If your social games are few, be content. Many contacts will not define you. Perhaps you've always had a limited number of friends and distanced yourself from many potential friendships. Perhaps you're too straightforward, simple, or honest. You've been lied to, taken advantage of, and betrayed.

You may have numerous acquaintances, but real friends will always be just a few people you love and trust. Be mindful about the size of your circle and understand the importance of quality over quantity when it comes to friendships. Don't fool yourself by holding on to the illusion that everyone is your friend. But also understand that not everyone is out to get you, hurt you, and dismiss you.

To find our path in life, we must dive into the moment. We must discard assumptions, expectations, and outside programming. It has never been about finding anything, but about noticing that we have everything we need to take the next step. There is no rush. No need to quit our job, to be famous or successful. We must accept where we are.

Work with what you have. Listen to what feels alive, magnetic, exciting, fascinating. Start your journey. Do what you can. Drop all expectations, because you do not know where life will take you. And if you do not resonate with what I have written, discard it. Look for the path that is already built within your soul.

It is true that those who are real tend to not have many friends. Genuine people are hard to find because they value deep, meaningful friendships. In doing so, they engage in deep connections that involve integrity, and they draw people with courage and moral principles. Unfortunately, most people are not real.

22. THE WIND

> *"Life is like the wind, calm and gentle. Then sudden gusts and great storms that blow."*

UNKNOWN

Have you ever closed your eyes and turned your face to the wind? Have you ever felt it sweep along your skin in an invisible ocean of exultation? That's the moment you know you are alive. I never know which cool gust of wind will enchant me, tousling my hair or my heart. I never know when it will stir my familiar ache of words.

What the wind brings, the wind also takes away. The wind can bring rain, a cold breeze, or damp and humid air. I never know which drop will kiss the trauma from my soul, reminding me all over again how I miss them better in the rain.

When the dunes of life march across the scene, they are formed from sand deposited by the wind. Then that sand somehow becomes cemented, locking the dunes in place. But the wind doesn't stop; it continues to blow from the same direction, eroding grooves and flutes into the cemented dunes.

Like life, our pieces erode through the gusts and breezes. We learn to collect and move forward, not knowing what lies ahead. Sometimes our path goes with the wind and other times against it. Through our journey of life, we learn to move along with the wind in search of our life's purpose. Sometimes the wind carries us forward effortlessly, filling our sails with purpose and direction, while other times it leaves us standing still, or even pushes backwards. Like leaves in the breeze, we're carried along paths we never expected, finding meaning in both the stillness and the storm.

23. LOST

"Not until we are lost do we begin to understand ourselves."

HENRY DAVID THOREAU

I feel as though I have spent the last few years wandering. Just when I think I have caught a glimpse of myself, it disappears as quickly as it appeared. I wouldn't say that time has been wasted because, as painful as it has been, I truly believe we must be lost sometimes to truly understand ourselves.

What is my purpose in life? Purpose can be defined as the reason for which something is done or created or for which something exists. When I find myself feeling lost in the woods with no way out, it slows me down. Then I start questioning what my motivation is in life.

Your purpose in life never changes. The clarity and the soul searching begins when you are at a loss. You are on a good path when you learn to accept yourself. To resolve your ambitions, you must know yourself on a deeper level. You must separate yourself from society to be more acquainted with your values. God will take you out of your life and make you feel empty because He wants you to turn to Him. It is in your state of perplexity where you will seek His guidance. He is sufficient for you, and you must place your trust in the Lord of the Magnificent Throne.

Try to be a better version of yourself today than you were yesterday. You don't want to reach the end and know that you have not lived a purpose-driven life. Make an impact on this world. Make a difference. Today, you will find your way out of the woods. Today you will know your destiny!

24. EXTRA TERRESTRIAL

"Two possibilities exist; either we are alone in the universe, or we are not. Both are equally terrifying."

ARTHUR C. CLARKE

Do you believe we are alone? With the vast universe, the question is not whether we are alone, but how many neighbors do we have? With billions of galaxies in the universe and millions of potential life-supporting planets, the possibility is promising. There is no guarantee that we could ever cross paths with life beyond our world. We may search for it, but the mystique will always be there. Contemplating this topic can be far beyond our mental capabilities. Utterly fascinating, mind blowing, and near impossible to fathom, can we also be the only bulb flickering in the darkness of our universe?

The notion that we may be alone in the universe is truly frightening. If the time comes and we no longer exist, what will the universe be like? If there are no other life-sustaining planets, how does that fundamentally affect how humanity understands itself?

What can be equally scary is the thought that there are other advanced beings in the universe. Are we destined to cross paths? It is more likely that we are not alone, and it fascinates us every time we look up at the sky and see the vast stars blanketing our horizon.

The observable universe is about 93 billion light years in diameter and is constantly expanding. It is in our human nature to explore and discover what our hearts desire. Perhaps our fate will lead us to find the truth, or maybe we are destined to never know. The vastness of space makes our outlook difficult, and its hostile environment represents an incredible challenge in our search for the truth. This remarkable amount of space can only be the work of a master creator and within lies the secret to our origins. In the end, only the Lord knows, and we know not.

25. SOLITUDE

"Some journeys are meant to be taken alone."

DARK NIGHT BEACON

I'd rather walk in the face of contempt, disbelief, and little support. I'd rather continue teetering on that edge until I reach solid ground by myself. Because it's true that some journeys I need to make alone. Alone, I can focus on myself, because no one else can give me the greatness

I seek. People disappoint me. They ignore me. They walk away from me. They let me down. They conjure excuses.

What if loneliness was not the enemy we thought, but a friend meant to lead us to God? Belief in our destiny is largely the art of renewing and reforming life, values, and experiences as God intended. My solitude is a reminder of the glory of what lies ahead for me with the Lord. In the stillness of being alone, we strip away the nose of the world and connect with our deeper selves. It is these quiet, introspective moments that we confront our desires, fears, and purpose.

Your voyage, your excursion, your trek must be made regardless of other's opinions. Nothing matters when you realize that you were always alone, always fending for yourself. Promises are too often broken. Commitments are not taken seriously. Disappointments are rampant. Although it's difficult to go forward without support, only strong souls will understand this concept. This journey is yours to take alone, because you are unique, and your destiny is at the control of your Creator.

26. THE VILLAIN

> *"And I know at last I'll be presented to the world as the villain, as the darkness in your story. All my efforts will be forgotten, and all my truths will be edited away. As you will narrate the tale of your rejected love."*

DARK NIGHT BEACON

I know that all my endeavors will be lost. I will be known as the miscreant. My veracity will be erased as they recount the story of their abandoned love. I wish things were different. I wish my situation was disparate, but I can't change the past. I can't undo the words that were said. I can't disengage the situations that led to my present state.

I want them to know that I was not present for the short term. I did not want a temporary ride. I've seen darkness and light. I have encountered the good and the bad. I was looking for peace, wanted nothing but tranquility and calm. I sought an angel on a journey to forever. I did not want anyone else but them.

It takes courage to write and illustrate the stance between good and evil. The core of one's character is a challenge to understand because we are all faced with grander interpretations. Sometimes we play our cards too close to our chest and unintentionally hold back the truth. While it creates confusion, some people will understand us and others simply will not. Those who do not will conjure a story to fit their means. They will make up for the lapses created by their minds—minds that were unable to understand your true intentions.

Some will see me as the villain. They are blind to my true intentions. They will come up with excuses and spread rumors to degrade my character. Little do they know that it is because of their misunderstanding that they have missed the opportunity to truly know me. Now that fate has diminished, it will lead me to the discovery of new possibilities ahead. Become the hero of your destiny and the champion of your tale. Be mature enough to know the truth and stay true to your morals and values because no one can take away who you are as a person unless you allow them to. Sometimes the most powerful response is no response at all.

27. THE DREAM

"Am I dreaming? No. I am living in my dream."

DARK NIGHT BEACON

When you sense liberation and freedom, the feeling of excitement, anticipation, and adventure will follow your path. Leave something that no longer serves you as you embark on a new journey. But as you transition to a new dream, you might also feel a tinge of sadness for what was left behind.

Deep in the forest of Hillsboro, a town located in Oregon, sits an airplane that has been modified into a home. Upon the greenery and in the trees, it is situated between a dream and an aspiration. Nestled in the meadows of love, it provides shelter for the dreamer. Perhaps it's an airplane for dreams to come true.

Are you thankful for what you have? Do you have your sights set to accomplish your dreams? These are the questions I asked myself as I explored this amazing airplane home. Gratitude fosters positive emotions, reducing stress, and strengthening relationships. By looking at your progress, you remind yourself of your capabilities and how far you've come. Aways appreciate the present and strive for future success. It will transform how you approach challenges by allowing you to see them as opportunities rather than obstacles.

You may not always be happy. You may not always have what you need. There are dreams that you will never fulfill. There are people you wish were in your life. There are stories you yearn to tell that will never be uttered. Your life is far from perfect. There are things you wanted to change, places you wanted to visit, a person you wanted to tell how you felt about but will probably never get that chance again.

Being thankful for what you have and making the best of what your Lord gave you is a dream. The dream of another tomorrow and the vision of a new day. You can fantasize what you wish your life could've been, but remember that God is the supreme planner. God's plan is for fresh inspiration, new views of spiritual reality, and spiritual growth. God's plan is for more heavenly good to be understood and experienced. Let God's plan lead the way and enjoy a beautiful day in the magical forest of the airplane.

28. THE RIVER

"A river cuts through a rock, not because of its power but because of its persistence."

JIM WATKINS

Persistence is a fundamental trait to develop in life because it is closely related to personal development and improvement. Like a river, your ability to grow and develop as a person will flow and nourish your success, wealth, and happiness. I've been grateful to see and swim in many rivers and it always reminds me of the tenacity of the human soul. It is the soul that manifests resilience, perseverance, and the ability to overcome adversity.

We all want success, but it requires persistence. Whether you want to lose a few pounds, do well in school, or obtain any goal that you want to succeed in, you must be persistent. If you want to obtain that promotion at work, you must give it all. The difference between a successful outcome and a failed one is giving up. Persistence is defined as the quality that allows someone to continue doing something even though it is difficult or opposed by others. This is not something you do with external goals; it is something you do internally. In the face of pain, agony, and defeat, it is difficult to stay persistent.

Know and accept that there will be obstacles and setbacks. Prepare for them. Nothing important was ever accomplished without adversity, complications, and difficulties. One of the ways you can prepare for issues and hindrances is to anticipate potential problems and develop a contingency plan. If things do not work out the way you hoped, review the steps you took and the process you followed. Reevaluate by examining what went wrong and where. Be flexible and experiment to see what techniques and strategies worked best to get where you want to go, and eventually, just like the river, you will cut through rock.

29. THE CHOSEN

"If your God entitles you to a specific land and justifies your existence as 'the chosen people', then you are no further than the devil himself."

DARK NIGHT BEACON

God is just. He loves all. He doesn't choose favorites, nor does He pick His most liked. His endearment is equal to all. His forgiveness is for all believers, on any continent, in any land, and in every corner of our universe. The Lord provided the land and sea for all. The world was created in perfect equilibrium. He raised heaven and established balance so that we would not transgress. God taught us to live with mutual love and affection and with humility. There is no distinction between race, color, national origin, sex, and age. There is love for all and hatred for none. Our fate in humanity is endearment.

If your God teaches you that you're supreme and above others, then it's not the message from your Creator. If your God justifies your existence through hate, divisiveness, and animosity, then it is not the way of your Supreme Lord. If your God promises a specific land to you, then you surely are a follower of Satan.

Anger and hate should be guarded against. Hatred is misfortune and self-destruction; overcome hate by love. There are some who say the devil is omnipresent. The devil lives in all of us. Why should we hate the devil if the monster inside of us helps us triumph over God? If we believe in the false ideology that we are loved more in the eyes of God than other people, we simply label Satan victorious.

Hate is a strong term that goes beyond simply disliking or disagreeing with someone. Hate means to will evil for another person, which is contrary to the law of love. We human beings are capable of great evil. Hatred is healthy when it inspires us to prayer and God-guided, compassion-informed action against it, even in ourselves. And we need not fear any of it, because evil is no match for the power of God.

God is everywhere by His knowledge and power, and nowhere, without being in a place, direction, or location, because He existed eternally before all the creations. The wrongdoers of today shall taste death, and when called upon to answer to their mischief, their eyes will stare in horror, because even love will be judged.

30. THE CAUSE

UNKNOWN

What transpired was meant to happen. What you endured was planned to ensue. If everything happens for a reason, do you find yourself struggling to understand why? In context to the sovereignty of our creator, Almighty God, His knowledge of all that is seen and concealed overrules all. He does whatever He chooses to, and all this takes precedence over reasoning. Nothing is in our control.

Nothing happens without His approval, knowledge, and will. Anything good or bad happens with His permission, and we should accept it as a blessing in disguise, since we cannot see or know what will happen from one moment to another in our lives. This leaves the burden of reasoning both on the faith and the faithful.

Things happen to us in life, and in the moment, we might not know why. But the notion that it happened for a reason empowers us, and how we create meaning is what matters most. We seek closure, mostly in cases of loss, and knowing the reasons satisfies us. But sometimes, when in search of closure, faith and the consolation of knowing there must be a reason behind the loss helps us move forward.

We can live our lives with good deeds and intentions. What happens next is out of our control. As humans, we lack the knowledge of our future and the unseen. All of us have experienced challenges in life. We have encountered obstacles and suffered setbacks. We have lost loved ones and been separated from others. We have stumbled and been through difficulty and complications. Trauma has consumed us. Trouble has devoured us. But have you noticed that nothing has stopped you? God's promise is that you will persevere, no matter the circumstance. As a believer, you are destined for greatness.

Looking back at why something happened to us often serves as an attempt to find meaning or closure. When we revisit painful or confusing events, we try to piece together reasons that explain the situation. Not everything has a clear cause or an easily identifiable reason. Some things just happen, and the meaning we assign to them may shift with time and perspective. Have you found that looking back offers clarity, or does it deepen the emotional weight? May your destination be full of peace, love, and surrounded by the grace of God.

CHAPTER VI

COMPASSION

When we feel connected to everything, we also feel responsible for everything. We become strong enough to love the world yet empty enough to watch its worst horrors. In this chapter, I wish for you to recognize that kindness lies in your heart. Coupled with mercy, they ultimately become the traits God seeks in humanity. Having the ability to forgive is arguably the most difficult challenge we face. But each time we forgive, we build courage and patience. In this chapter, you will see how forgiveness can become a blessed way to live. I invite you to expand your mind on the promise that the Lord will forgive you, if you forgive them.

1. MADNESS

> *"Understand me. I'm not like an ordinary world. I
> have my madness. I live in another dimension, and
> I do not have time for things that have no soul."*

CHARLES BUKOWSKI

Comprehending your character can be a daunting task. Grasping your behavior can be challenging. Deciphering your intentions can be difficult. You are not like the others who make their time available to be sucked dry of any hope to win the battles in their minds. You fight too hard every day to erase, remember, and overcome the thoughts in your mind.

We should be kind to one another, for everyone we meet is fighting an internal battle. We are reminded daily by brief encounters, private messages, emails, texts, or comments on social media that we are not alone, and we are all different. Remember, we all deserve understanding.

The next time you meet someone, remember that they are also battling something. It can be difficulty in school, work, a strain in the family or relationship. They may be battling internal demons. They might be facing a deadline, a challenge, a complex goal, or the loss of something meaningful to them. Be patient, be helpful, and most importantly, be understanding. You never know when you might change someone's life in a positive way.

Have an open mind, a loving heart, and a welcoming attitude. You may not please everyone, but the important ones will be thankful for your generosity, your care, and your love. God has promised that your sacrifice in helping the less fortunate, the vulnerable, and the helpless will one day be rewarded.

2. VENGEANCE

"Vengeance blackens the soul. I've always feared that I would become that which I fought against. I walk the edge of the abyss every night, but I haven't fallen in, and I thank God for that."

ALFRED PENNYWORTH

Many people would rather see me revert to disbelief now that I believe. This is due to jealousy on their part, after the truth has become evident to them. I shall pardon them, and leave them alone, until God issues His judgment. God is omnipotent.

What do you think the proper response should be for people who wish us ill? People who want to see us abandon God, to see us disbelieve? If you want to get vengeance, become a better person. Spend the energy on improving your soul. The rewards will be far greater. Would you lend God a loan of righteousness to have it repaid multiplied a thousandfold? God is the One who provides and withholds, and to Him you will be returned.

We spend precious hours dwelling on how we were wronged. You can't believe they did that. How can you retaliate? If instead we spend that time making ourselves better, not only will we be better off spiritually but also emotionally and mentally. When we hold on to anger and resentment, we are only hurting ourselves. Holding onto anger is like holding a hot coal with the intention of throwing it at someone else. Righteousness is the solution to all our problems, not retribution.

I understand the concept of vengeance. After all, I was wronged at a vulnerable young age. I understand the fine line without crossing it. I know that vengeance can lead to evil, and that God is always watching us. He is the giver of justice. I realize that avengement and reprisal may not always be the appropriate response. This understanding is what separates me from the rest.

3. RIGHTEOUSNESS

"Learn to do right; Seek justice. Defend the oppressed. Take up the cause of the fatherless; Plead the case of the widow."

HOLY BIBLE, 117

Always be good, even when no one is watching. Be pro-active. Defend those who are persecuted, abused, and subjugated. Help those victimized and assist the suppressed. Strive for righteousness. I understand this concept because I have been through this circumstance in my own life, in my own profession. I believe victims are the most vulnerable souls, and I go to great lengths to ensure their safety. Going through a traumatic experience was life-changing. My perception of the world changed. I don't want anyone to feel what it's like to be oppressed.

God requires us to act justly, love mercifully, and walk humbly before Him. When faced with choices, we must consider what God desires. But He doesn't want us to merely do what is right. He wants us to learn to do right so that we can live purely and wisely, a life where no evil finds expression in any part of our story.

Doing good deeds is a task tied with faith. We don't act to receive something in return. We behave this way because we fear God. It is a characteristic of good self-esteem and wellbeing. We must stand up or speak up for the truth when freedom can be brought to those around us. We must love one another with our whole hearts and grow together. We must be peacemakers on Earth and show God that we can serve His purpose. If living a life of good cause, peace, and joy doesn't fulfill your soul, I don't know what will.

4. THE PROMISE

"Sleep the night with not an ounce of hatred or envy;
for God promised to forgive you, if you forgive them."

UNKNOWN

Our relationships contain many people with the potential to hurt us, very often in small, ongoing ways. Sometimes, in trying to be good people, we brush these hurts aside. We act like they don't bother us, but they do. Our egos are like magnets, and resentments are attracted to them. We need to forgive as often as we sin. Forgiveness is holy and should have no limits. Clemency should be eternal and timeless. The Lord promises that tolerance is possible, even when hurt seems too great to repair.

We experience a heart of stone when we are too angry, selfish, or frozen by the pain others have caused us. A heart of flesh, while it may be vulnerable, is compassionate. Our soul sees that while we are feeling pain, the other person may also be hurting for that pain they caused us. We can get so caught up in ourselves that we do not even notice another is struggling from the offense. It is true that people need to be held accountable for their actions, but these people also need our patience.

When we forgive others, we are no longer restrained by our own anger. It moves us from our selfish illusions to an appealing reality. Letting go of the fantasy that we can change the past is difficult. When we can change others, or change ourselves, it allows us to grow closer to our Lord with remorse and forgiveness. It allows room for God to help us ward off the resentment we feel.

Each time we forgive, it paves the way for the next time. Practicing courage and patience and letting the Lord into the process of forgiveness is like exercising a muscle; it grows stronger and stronger. Together with Him, we can reach a point where forgiveness is intuitive, a blessed way to live. So, pardon them, for your Lord promised to exonerate you.

5. STARTING ANEW

> *"Be soft. Do not let the world make you hard. Do not let the pain make you hate. Do not let the bitterness steal your sweetness. Take pride that even though the rest of the world may disagree, you still believe it to be a beautiful place."*

IAIN THOMAS

Life is always a struggle, whether internally or externally. Humankind is undeniably connected. Learning to cope with the events that take place, whether they affect you on a personal level or not, is the key to pushing through the struggle. Keep your mind and your heart open. Being judgmental and critical of others only depletes you of precious energy and time. Have compassion for others and be gentle with yourself because you are worthy of love.

It's okay to be bitter and resentful, but it doesn't define you. Holding onto hatred and resentment is toxic and won't change anything. It will, however, hinder your ability to find peace within. You may have endured personal pain. You may even hate yourself at times for the pain you caused others. Hate can control your life and suffocate you. Hating the other person truly only gives them satisfaction. Let go of those who are negative entities in your life. Much like hatred, bitterness can steal your sweetness and your ability to be compassionate. Holding on to it does absolutely nothing but give the other person the satisfaction of seeing you miserable. Let it go, forgive, and move on.

There is beauty all around us. Hatred and resentment cloud our vision and only allow for one view of our surroundings, which is generally not all that pretty. We must forgive, be compassionate, and let go of those who bring us down. We must surround ourselves with those who lift us up. If you are rebuilding your life or starting anew, create a foundation of positive affirmations and self-love. Surround yourself with people who will keep your soul illuminated. Most importantly, love yourself, know your self-worth, set boundaries, and forgive yourself. That is when you will find ultimate peace and success.

6. THE SMILE

"Smile; it is the key that fits the lock of everybody's heart."
ANTHONY J. DANGELO

I don't smile very often. As a matter of fact, it's rare that others will find me grinning. It's not because I am not happy or sad. Its absence is a mystery, one that makes even me wonder why it doesn't present itself more often.

God created mankind with an innate inclination to love those who are friendly. A person who meets others with a smile drives away their anxiety and troubles and spreads tranquility and comfort. This is because smiling is a commendable characteristic, and the one who smiles is complimented. You may not be able to satisfy someone with your wealth, but you can always satisfy them with your cheerfulness. A simple good deed like smiling goes a long way as an act of charity.

A smile is the light in your window that tells others that there is a caring, sharing person inside. Everyone loves a society full of love and peace. We hardly have to move a muscle to smile, but the effect a smile has is tremendous. It can lessen tense situations. Smile, and the world will grin back at you. Smile at nature and it will beam back at you. Smiling is a good way to express pleasure. Actions speak louder than words, and smiles can win hearts.

A genuine grin can make you approachable and trust-worthy. It exudes an aura of warmth and positivity. If you ever find yourself having difficulty smiling, remember that if you truly knew God's purpose in your life, you would laugh a little and weep often. It doesn't mean your smile is gone; your act of devotion for His love is so great that you can't help but to turn to Him in times of sorrow. And when you shed a tear, God will turn your sadness into a garden of smiles.

The God of mercy comes from a wellspring of unfathomable love. His endless compassion is a highlight of His guidance and forgiveness. It is the reason why He is always ready to forgive sins and responds to prayers. The ability to feel with others as expressions of interconnected oneness reflects the unity of God. I hope you find it in your heart to love often, forgive frequently, and be thankful to your Lord with a daily smile.

7. COMPANIONSHIP

"The moon understands what it means to be human. Uncertain. Alone. Cratered by imperfections."

TAHEREH MAFI

The moon is a loyal companion. It's always there, watching, steadfast, knowing us in our light and dark moments, changing forever just as we do. Every day it's a different version of itself. Sometimes it is weak and wan and other times it is strong and full of light.

The moon will never abandon us. Whether we are awake or asleep, it is always there. It revolves around us to guide us through the night with its brightness. It dwells in darkness as it reigns over our world, glowing in its full splendor to those willing to look up. There is something haunting in the light of the moon; it has the tranquility of an intangible soul, an inconceivable mystery.

Allow the light of the moon to touch you with a sense of tremendous compassion. Unlike the sun, its light is gentle, beautiful, soothing, and nurturing. The mood of the moon awakens the mind, delighting in your presence and pouring wisdom, confidence, and nobility into you. Human character can be compared to the moon in many ways. We change our emotions, appearance, and attitude every day, just like the moon does. Even something so beautiful as the moon has its imperfections.

As humans, we are susceptible to sin. It is a natural part of being human. God never created us to be perfect, faultless, and incapable of evil. Understanding that you will never achieve perfection in this world proves God's immense compassion. We are constantly in need and our dependence relies solely on the Lord to provide. This dependence should humble a person, like the moon. There is great wisdom in the comparison of the moon and humankind. Simply look up at the cosmos and let its rays touch your soul.

8. PETS

"Until one has loved an animal, a part of one's soul remains unawakened."

ANATOLE FRANCE

Many of us are pet owners. Our animals are a part of our family. We hold them dear to our hearts. Some are our companions; others are there to guide those who have special needs. Those who do not have a connection to a pet might find it difficult to understand this special bond between a pet and its owner.

We should all have a special love for animals. When there is an injustice done to us, we have a voice and resources to air our complaints. Animals have few advocates. We destroy their homes to build ours; we destroy their hunting grounds for food. When they wander into our territory in search of food, we call them pests and kill or trap them.

Those who love animals have broadened their minds. You can do no wrong in the animal's eyes. You become a companion, best friend, protector, teacher, and provider, and the animal will be happy to spend their life trying to please you. Compassion and mercy should not only encompass humanity but also extend to all creatures in the world.

There's something profound about having a deep and affectionate connection to an animal of another species. Have they awakened your soul? It is difficult to trust a human who is indifferent to animals and impossible to trust one who is cruel to them.

9. SUFFERING

> *"Human beings are members of a whole, in*
> *creation of one essence and soul. If one member*
> *is afflicted with pain, other members uneasy*
> *will remain. If you have no sympathy for human*
> *pain, the name of human you cannot retain."*

SAADI SHIRAZ

Pain is the one and only true evil. Why emphasize pain and other forms of suffering rather than pleasure and happiness? Pain is much more powerful than pleasure. Would you rather avoid an hour's torture than gain an hour's bliss?

Our concern for the pain and distress of others should be extended to anything that feels pain, regardless of their sex, class, race, religion, nationality, or species. Many moral principles and ideals have been proposed over the centuries, such as justice, freedom and equality. But these are mere steppingstones to the ultimate good, which is happiness. And happiness is made easier by freedom from all forms of pain and suffering.

Success, when fueled by compassion, tends to be inclusive, empathetic, and impactful. It moves beyond personal gain and seeks to elevate others along the way. Together, they create a balance that benefits both individuals and the communities they touch. I want you to leave a legacy that is respected and admired by adopting stronger morale, and greater loyalty.

The reason why other ideals are considered important is because people believe they are essential to the banishment of suffering. We must always show sympathy and understanding to all those living around us. Compassion is what separates humans from other species. The power of empathy has been granted to us by our Creator and we shall show one another the care and understanding we all deserve.

10. EXPECTATIONS

"Do good without expecting anything in return."

HOLY QURAN, 74-6

Generosity is a virtuous trait that every person should strive to attain. For the believer who closely adheres to the teachings of God, kindness and giving from what they have becomes part of their good character. Generosity is the opposite of greed, and stinginess is a disease of the heart. We should avoid this substandard quality, for it is a source of corruption. Faith and righteous deeds purify the heart, so we must be outstretched, giving to those in need.

A generous person shares what they have with others, thinking of others as they think of themselves. We benefit by helping others and solving their problems. We make people happy and prevent them from doing wrong, which is often a direct result of poverty. This is a great service to society, and there are some people who spend their lives in this service, establishing valuable foundations which remain after them, such as hospitals and libraries.

When your intention is purely to alleviate another's suffering or offer help, without any personal gain, you represent a rare kind of unconditional kindness. Give without any expectations but recognize when you need to preserve your own emotional well-being. When effort and kindness go unacknowledged, it can trigger feelings of being invisible or unappreciated, which can affect one's self worth.

Whether giving in abundance from our riches or a small amount from our meager means, one should give with complete satisfaction, with the best of intentions, and without expecting anything in return. Be kind to others not expecting anything in return but hoping to please the Almighty Lord. When you give up something for His sake, you will be compensated with something better.

11. THE HUNTER

> *"Until the lion learns how to write, every story will glorify the hunter."*

AFRICAN PROVERB

There are unknown realities in the forest when a lion and a hunter come face to face. The lion, considered the king of the jungle and the most powerful animal, symbolizes all animals. Hunters are powerful and respected in their communities. They are believed to have some supernatural powers. They often have exceptional stories to tell that emphasize their achievements and their hunting skills. People often praise them and celebrate their exploits. This is especially true when they come home with feared animals like lions.

Even though people celebrate their stories, they are also aware that they will never know the details of the battles fought in the forest. When a hunter brings home an animal, it may very well be due to the hunter's skills, but it may also be due to pure luck. The animal might have been sleeping or injured. No matter in what circumstances the animal is killed, a hunter will always tell a story that makes them shine. Is the hunter telling the true story or just bragging? No one will ever know.

There is a unique struggle between the lion and the hunter because we all know well that a story is never complete until one hears it from both sides. The one who does not have the voice is often the loser. This underachiever might well be the lion to the hunter, the servant to the master, or the chief to his subjects. It is in these circumstances, when one voice dominates the other, that this proverb is often heard.

There is a story behind every word, every letter, every sentence. Never listen to random opinions of others; it's not true until you see it with your own eyes and hear it with your own ears. Never make assumptions. We must treat each other with consideration and sensitivity, for we will all be judged one day on our actions and how we treat our fellow beings and animals.

12. TIME

"The greatest gift you can give to someone is your time."

RICK WARREN

Your time is your life. In the midst of our living, time continues its endless journey. Time is a gift, though we rarely acknowledge it as such. Every day, time is equally allotted to everyone, and what we do with that time is up to us. We can spend our time wisely or worthlessly. We can squander it or invest it. We can enjoy it or abuse it. We can live it or retreat from it, but it moves on regardless.

Time cannot be contained; only the memories caught within that time can be. We have the amazing ability to capture within our memory bank those moments that fill us with adrenaline, love, passion, peace, and a revealing awareness of who we are as individuals.

Time gives us opportunities to make changes within ourselves that empower us to be better human beings. To seek forgiveness for wrongs we've incurred and seek to forgive, to change how we see others and how we view ourselves. Time adds value and builds our self-esteem, which will ultimately have a positive effect on those around us.

Time cannot be seen. A clock is used as a gauge to keep us aware of what we need to do and when we need to do it. Within the sphere of time, we can do whatever we want, but using effectively is time well spent. Unconsciously, we decide daily how we're going to spend our time. Let's spend it wisely by creating memories that will benefit us and those we'll touch.

We need to use the time we have to live in the now, to embrace good, to love ourselves unconditionally, and to give life to others by showing we care. Time is too precious to waste, so use the time given to you wisely. You will not only find fulfillment but enjoyment in the process. When you give someone your time, you are giving them a portion of your life that you'll never get back. Time is precious because you only have a set amount of it. You can make more money, but you can't make more time.

13. THE WIZARD

"Sometimes the universe explodes out of your muzzle."

DARK NIGHT BEACON

Magic or miracles are what we call the transformations we cannot yet explain. The important thing is to understand you are part of the miracle, just like the seed that will germinate only if the ground is fertile. Each one tends to their own garden, and if no work is done, no rose will blossom. The sun and rain are available to everyone, but the sowing is personal and nontransferable. It is essential to understand that everyone must play their part in order to be dazzled by the magic of life.

Do honorable deeds; do not wait for others to do them. To love unconditionally is an act of great wisdom, as it brings the expansion of consciousness, the liberation of the soul, and permission to see in the dark. Become a better person each day. Be aware of the power that lies dormant in the core of your being.

The thought of the cosmos bursting out first came to fruition when I went to the shooting range. The bullet speeding out of the muzzle caused an explosion as the primer on the cartridge ignited and burned. In less than a tenth of a second and lasting mere milliseconds, this astonishing burst of light appeared and quickly disappeared. Its beauty could only be seen from a perfectly timed photo at the right angle and lighting.

Remember that you are the wizard. The magic is when we transform ourselves; we change the world with exceedingly small, daily miracles that only the keen eye can see. We see the transformations overflow naturally, from the twinkle in the eyes, the loving sensibility in the feelings, the enlightened and clear thoughts free from automatisms, the good word, from compassion for the lack of understanding, and from acting composed and dignified.

The universe itself is a miracle. It appeared out of nowhere when there was no time, space, or matter in existence. We are a being devoid of any morality. Facing the hurdles of everyday life, we expand with knowledge and spread righteousness so that our hearts will resonate with pure light. It is a crucial step where traces of individual evolution become part of the spirit, like a twinkling star in the sky that, little by little, lightens everything and everyone, in sync with the expansion of the universe itself until it is entirely engulfed.

14. FEELINGS

"You can close your eyes to the things you don't want to see, but you can't close your heart to the things you don't want to feel."

JOHNNY DEPP

We can easily close our eyes and choose not to see something we don't want to see. However, emotions and feelings from the heart cannot be easily ignored. We can't just switch that off. We must fight it if we want to let it go. It is a battle not easily won, one that can turn our perception of the entire world around. Is that why I see the world in a dark gloom?

Selective ignoring is a human talent, and necessary for focusing on selected importance. But on a deeper level, the things you choose to ignore will often remain with you. Any feelings that you lock out for the sake of expediency, fear, or distaste are likely to resurface at some point.

The best but sometimes most challenging solution is to be willing to feel anything, and face those feelings calmly. When you do this, they can no longer exercise any command over your actions. You become the owner rather than the captive of such feelings, able to have them or not at will. Feeling things at such a deep level means we are empathetic and sensitive.

My heart may never let go of the deep pain from my past trauma. No matter what I do, for the rest of my life, this emotion will forever stay with me. Even with my eyes closed, I vividly remember that unfortunate situation. For some of us, the same emotion of love will also remain forever in our hearts. Be grateful for every feeling that you endure in life because it is God's way to encourage you to not only embrace those emotions but to also grow closer to Him.

15. TOLERANCE

"Your compassion is a weakness your enemies will not share."

HENRI DUCARD

Our compassion becomes the villain's strength. The more we care, the stronger the evil souls become. Our sympathy, kindness, and humanity are important. It separates us from them. We show sensitivity. We garner the emotion of warmth, love, and mercy. They show indifference and cruelty. They use our empathy to become apathetic. They take advantage of our kindness. Don't ever play any part of their game.

When we show tolerance, it can lead to being taken advantage of or harmed. Are you willing to be more compassionate knowing the possibility of being exploited by others? Do you believe in second chances? Would you allow someone to regain your trust after they took advantage of your vulnerability? Compassion is a strength that can foster understanding, cooperation, and support. After all, showing empathy is what makes us human.

Every hurt believer will eventually face a choice of whether to forgive as they recall their relationship with someone who hurt them deeply. Forgiveness is the ultimate resolution to unwanted loss or grief. It's a choice to make peace when you don't get what you want. If we accept our decree, we are no longer fighting with our emotions. We learn to submit wholeheartedly to what we cannot control.

We must all show this compassion to those who we may dislike for whatever reason. We must forgive. We must make amends, reparation, and recompensation. Compassion is an attribute of God. This divine quality serves as a model for human behavior, encouraging believers to act with kindness and empathy, even when we know we will be hurt. We must show leniency because only God can judge us.

16. HATE

> *"Don't pursue something with a vengeful heart,
> or it will destroy you. Hate wraps a cold hand
> around your heart and hollows you out."*

DANNIKA DARK

I believe in rehabilitation and tolerance. I believe every soul can heal, learn, and repent. Everyone deserves a second chance. But hate seems to always sneak around the corner. The negative experiences in my life have consumed part of my mind in abomination. But through all the hostility and aversion, I still find it in my heart to have hope for others. Even through all the disappointments, I look for the good in people.

We love to hate others, and that is why we are emotionally incompetent. Many people don't use their voices to make things better. They express their opinions simply to hurt others, to silence opposite thoughts. The hatred we see daily is doing us no good as a society. Our hearts have become completely incompetent, and hate has taken over our emotions. Hating others is an effortless way out. It is a self-defense mechanism. When under attack, the ability to quickly separate foes from friends is essential to survive. However, most of our current threats are perceived ones, not real ones. We create fights, confrontations, disputes, and drama.

When things don't go well, we blame others and look for a scapegoat. We want to be right and feel safe. We embrace hate to protect our self-esteem or to defend our community's interests and beliefs. People hate what they don't understand. They reject those who think or look differently. People hate others because of what they reflect about them too. When someone attacks you, avoid getting into a useless battle.

No one wins the war of hatred. The world benefits from diversity. If we all look, think, believe, feel, and act the same, the world would be boring. Understanding, tolerance, and self-awareness are critical to moving from a defensive to an acceptive mode. It's not easy. Being tolerant is one of our most significant challenges as human beings. It starts by accepting our uniqueness so we can allow others to be true to themselves too.

God has encouraged His believers to show forgiveness. We should all show this compassion to those who have different thoughts or opinions. Learn to find beauty in what looks different. Most importantly, have hope for a better tomorrow, a better person who can learn from yesterday's mistakes and grow into a better future.

17. UNTYING

> *"Some of us think holding on makes us
> strong; but sometimes it is letting go."*

HERMANN HESSE

To truly live in the present, one must let go of the past. That does not mean forgetting what has occurred, but instead remembering and accepting it. Memories may have the power to overtake us, but we also have the power to use them. Are you still working toward accepting what happened in your past? Are you proud of yourself for trying to improve?

Life can be difficult to navigate, especially when you are carrying a part of someone else in your heart. There is always hope when you choose to focus on the good. You hope for their return, but you try to lighten the load day by day. After all, acceptance is a process, not a sudden state of being. It was never really saying goodbye that you had an issue with, nor was it losing those close to you. The hardest part was what was left after the fact. The hardest part was knowing that it would never really be over, and that the goodbye was not the grand finale you had hoped for.

You spent months gathering evidence for what you had done wrong, reversing time in your mind and replaying scenarios to figure out how to fix it. There was, of course, no way to resolve this issue. Maybe you did the best you could and held on longer than most people would have, yet you still hung onto what happened, never letting yourself forget the small mistakes you made.

Perhaps you shouldn't be holding on. Maybe you should find the courage to let go. Letting go can also be an act of love. If you can't give the person you love what they need to feel truly happy and fulfilled, it's only with the utmost love that you'll be able to let them go. Your Lord wants you to surrender to a state of consciousness that leads to mental, emotional, and physical peace. It is the only road to wholeness, contentment, and fulfillment you seek in life. Perhaps the art of letting go is another form of love that you'll always carry in your heart.

18. THE VISION

"Your vision will become clear only when you can look into your own heart. Who looks outside, dreams; who looks inside, awakes."

CARL JUNG

To look inside is to look at our conflicts, fears, anxieties, repressed emotions, pleasures, and our attachments. To peek inside our thoughts is to see our greed, anger, jealousies, pride, suffering, and our loneliness. All the things we have been holding on to or hiding from are within us. To look means to observe. Actions are automatic and choiceless if our observation is complete, sincere, and without division.

We hold on to these things by projecting a dream from our memory to an alternate reality and not the one in our direct experience. We project stories, fantasies, beliefs and ideals so we don't have to see the reality in front of us.

Perhaps you could see the error you were making, and it was pointing you to face reality and not hide from it. Maybe beyond the projection lies reality, and beyond the perceived reality lies something fantastic that cannot be perceived. Thoughts cannot be known because we have been holding onto or hiding from them. We need to find out for ourselves; it's the only way we can find the truth about us.

By observing your heart, you will see how thought creates psychological time to keep the illusion alive. You will see how thought created you—the personality, the sum of worries, anxiety, pleasure, attachments, and greed.

Awaken your aching heart. Let it be free to pursue what it truly desires. Don't allow anything or anyone to stop you from what you believe in. Extend loving benignity to yourself. Startle the innate intelligence that sits concealed in the warmth of your heart. Like the meeting of a beacon piercing the darkness, a warm glow emerges from the abyss of the night. Establish your dominance of your mind's hierarchy like the shine of a lighthouse. Only then will you understand love and kindness and see the good in others.

19. THE THRONE

*"On the highest throne in the world, we
still sit only on our own bottom."*

MICHEL DE MONTAIGNE

When one sits on their throne in the world, they are in a position of power, authority, and influence. It implies that they have achieved a level of success and recognition that sets them apart from the rest of society. This concept of a "throne" can be metaphorical, representing a position of leadership in a particular field or industry, or it can be literal, as in the case of a monarch or ruler.

Sitting on one's throne in the world comes with great responsibility. Those who hold this position are expected to make wise decisions, lead with integrity, and serve as role models for others. They are responsible for setting the tone and direction of their organization, community, or even their country. Their actions and decisions have a ripple effect that can impact countless lives.

However, with great power comes great scrutiny. Those who sit on their throne in the world are constantly under the microscope, with their every move and decision being analyzed and criticized by the public. They must be prepared to face the consequences of their actions and take responsibility for any mistakes or missteps.

Despite the challenges, sitting on one's throne can be incredibly rewarding. It offers the opportunity to make a positive impact on the world, to inspire others and leave a lasting legacy. It is a position of privilege but also one of great responsibility. In the end, whether one is sitting on a literal throne or a metaphorical one, it is important to remember that true leadership is not about power or control but about service and humility. The most effective leaders are those who lead by example, who listen to the needs of their community and work tirelessly to make the world a better place for all.

20. ANIMAL WORLD

*"Animals are simply magical creatures, and they can
teach us more than we can ever teach them."*

DARK NIGHT BEACON

Often, people and animals enjoy each other's company.
When people adopt domesticated animals into their families as pets, animals give humans the blessings of companionship and a magical connection. In the wild, people show their love to animals by taking care of the environment the animals depend upon to survive, and wild animals reward humans with displays of their God-given beauty and power. But beyond those common bonds of love, God may bring people and animals together in miraculous ways.

Animals may also help people who have gone through emotional trauma make miraculous recoveries. They give those people unconditional love and encourage them to regain hope and confidence. Animals can miraculously improve the quality of life for people who are disabled or recovering from a physical illness or injury. Many organizations train animals to perform a wide variety of helpful tasks for people with special physical needs.

Find it in your heart to care for all animals. They are innocent souls with a special bond reserved in their nucleus. They are creations of God. The Lord urges us to be kind to His creatures and therefore kind to ourselves. Your compassion is a sign of what truly lies in your heart. Kindness and mercy are two of the most important traits God seeks in humanity. One of the most important rights that belongs to animals is that they are entitled to our good treatment.

21. ETHICS

*"The greatest ethical test that we're ever going to face
is the treatment of those who are at our mercy."*

LYN WHITE

Good morals is an eternal divinity that very few possess. There are times in life when we encounter someone who is less fortunate than us. They may not be blessed with the things that are present in our lives. We must decide whether to lend them a hand or walk away. Displaying good character is a virtuous trait that every person should strive to attain. As for the believer who closely adheres to the teachings of God, kindness and giving are a part of one's good character.

Generosity is the opposite of stinginess, as stinginess is a disease of the heart. We should avoid this inferior quality, for it is a source of corruption. Faith and righteous deeds purify the heart, so we should be outstretched, giving to those in need.

Treating those who are at our mercy reflects our true character. Whether in positions of power, authority, or simply in moments where we have the upper hand, how we choose to behave reveals a great deal about our values and sense of humanity. The ability to show empathy and kindness, especially when it's easy to act otherwise, elevates our moral standing. Compassion softens power and can help foster healing and reconciliation in those who are vulnerable.

Holding power often presents the temptation to dominate or degrade others. History is rife with examples of individuals and systems exploiting this dynamic, often justified by convenience, fear, or superiority. True strength lies not in control or humiliation but in empowering those who are weaker. By treating people with dignity, even when they are in a vulnerable position, we contribute to building a more just and humane society.

Ultimately, how you treat those at your mercy often reverberates through time. Acts of cruelty can breed resentment, retaliation, and cycles of violence. Acts of kindness can build trust, gratitude, and lasting peace. Exploring how you behave when you hold power over others can offer a profound lens through which to examine your moral choices.

22. THE HORSE

"We have almost forgotten how strange a thing it is that something so huge and powerful and intelligent an animal as a horse should allow another, and far more feeble animal, to ride upon its back."

PETER GRAY

Trust is essential to forming and maintaining social attachments. When people are in trusting relationships, they are healthier, happier, and more productive. Trust involves giving up control and accepting vulnerability with the expectation of being protected from harm. Trustworthy people are consistent and compassionate and can be relied on to safeguard the best interests of others. Importantly, trust is only earned and tested when an individual is at risk of physical harm or emotional distress.

Horses let humans ride them because a relationship of trust is developed through hard work, time, and training. In the wild, horses run when humans attempt to approach them. Most people buy horses trained to ride and don't put much thought into why a horse lets them sit on their back. We train them to allow us to ride them, but there is a reason we ride horses and not zebras. Horses have a disposition that is agreeable to being domesticated. We have domesticated horses for thousands of years. When treated with kindness and respect, horses respond brilliantly.

Be grateful when you climb on your horse's back that it allows you to ride freely. Kind and consistent training is imperative if you want a partnership with your horse. Harmonious communication and physical coordination between horses and humans relies on mutual trust and cooperation. Leaders gain trust by demonstrating competence and ability, showing kindness and goodwill, and making an emotional connection with others. To earn a horse's trust, people can model these qualities by using consistent and skilled handling techniques, developing sensitivity to the horse's emotional state, and responding to the horse in a gentle, fair, and forgiving manner.

23. EMOTION

"I've learned that people will forget what you said, people will forget what you did, but people will never forget how you made them feel."

MAYA ANGELOU

It is important how you make people feel. If you want to do something important and significant in life, then focus on doing something that makes people feel good, important, valued, loved, and respected. Make them feel special. We typically make decisions based on emotion and feelings, then later try to justify that decision with logic. How you make people feel has an impact from the first time you interact with them. That initial interaction may be through a smile, a small generosity, or another positive means of reciprocity.

People may not always agree with you or your ideas. From time to time, they're bound to have experiences with you that are sub-optimal, but they must always feel that you understand them, respect them, and strive to be there when needed. Keep this in mind when you are building friendships that you are planning your next getaway and adventure. Remember that people will never forget how you make them feel. Whether you are good to them or bad, they will always recollect those moments.

No matter what happens or how bad it seems today, life does go on, and it will be better tomorrow. Regardless of your relationship with those you love, you'll miss them when they're gone from your life. Whenever you have pain, you don't have to be one. Reach out and touch someone every day. People love a warm hug or just a friendly pat on the back.

We all still have a lot to learn. What we say is less important than how we say it, and what we do is less important than how we do it. It's how we say it and how we do it that will make the biggest impact. And no matter how much time may pass, it's how we made them feel that they will remember.

24. THE MASK

> *"People are mad because they must wear a
> mask. I've been wearing one my entire life."*

DARK NIGHT BEACON

The COVID-19 pandemic that caused a worldwide outbreak in early 2020 changed our worldviews. We were forced to wear masks to reduce the number of germs that we exhaled into the environment around us. This was one way to prevent the spread of germs. Unfortunately, some were terribly upset at this inconvenience. But I can assure you that throughout the history of epidemic responses, every measure we take to combat illness has a downside or united consequence.

It is true that you are living someone else's dream. There is someone out there in the world right now who is less fortunate. When they close their eyes and dream of the perfect life, they picture your current situation. What you have, what you do, your freedom, and many other things. Given the chance, they would swap places with you in a heartbeat. Think about that before you complain about something today. You have it so good.

Wearing a mask to help stop the spread of the deadly virus COVID-19 may be an inconvenience. The thought of putting one on may take away your time from doing something more worthwhile. But have you ever imagined how many lives a simple mask has saved? There are millions of people who do not even have the luxury of possessing a mask. Imagine living in a world where at any moment you can catch this lethal infection knowing it could have been prevented. Now think of someone you love, how they may be taken away from you because someone felt that wearing a mask was not worth the trouble.

Like many life skills, we must be taught how to look at the world through a lens of gratitude. We need to understand that the people we're helping are no different at the core than we are. They've just been dealt a harder lot in life.

Developing empathy can shape us into the great people we want to become. Wear that mask proudly. Together we can overcome future viruses and save the human species from destruction. Perhaps it can even prepare us for a deadlier virus coming soon. A global pandemic is one that should be taken seriously. I am glad the pandemic is finally over, and we can breathe.

25. THE SEA

"I found myself in a sea in which the waves of joy and sorrow were clashing against each other."

NAGUIB MAHFOUZ

In fluid and dynamic motion, ocean waves form as wind blows across the surface of the ocean, creating small ripples that eventually become waves with increasing time and distance. When waves reach shallow water, they become unstable and begin to break, imposing large hydrodynamic forces on organisms living in these regions. Waves in the ocean can travel thousands of miles and see no boundaries, nations, or latitudes. Their destiny is to meet a coastline.

During your visits to the beach, did you notice the amazing grace of the waves as their demanding presence rose dramatically? An ocean wave is a miracle. It's an inimitable, magical, and singular creation that, despite being short-lived, changes all living beings. Waves are like humans. Each one of them was, is, and will be a unique, exclusive, and unrepeatable entity. They can be unstable, violent, and chaotic but also delicate, gentle, kind, and smooth like us. Waves defy us constantly and inevitably but also soothe our minds. They're an unsolvable paradox that is comparable to our own behavior.

A wave has a beginning, a middle, and an end, just like any human. A wave's mission is to travel and change the space where it moves, from birth to death. Just because a wave crashes and disappears doesn't mean it doesn't have a purpose.

There is nothing in the world that brings me peace at a time of solitude than ocean waves. Many find that the tune of the ocean waves resembles the melody in our own hearts. It is the place I most often visit when sorrows appear. May your joy be as deep as the ocean and your sorrow be as light as its tides.

Allow your grief to rise like the tides of the ocean. There will be times when you will collapse in sorrow and pain, but there will also be times when you will laugh like the abundance of the sea. Do not ask to be different and do not pray to be like others. You will always love your life in the sea of joy and sorrow because there is no life without.

26. THE ARCH

> *"An arch consists of two weaknesses which, leaning one against the other, make a strength."*

LEONARDO DA VINCI

In order for a friendship to last, two people must learn to be like the two sides of an arch and lean into each other for strength. When I came across the Delicate Arch, located in Moab, Grand County, Utah, I began to think about how it was made and where it generated its strength to stand in the unforgiving land of Arches National Park. At 52 feet tall, it is considered one of the most recognized geological features in the world.

The definition of an arch is typically a curved structural member spanning an opening and serving as a support, like door frames or bridge supports. An arch holds up things like walls or bridges and can also be a covering or a protection in things like arbors or pergolas. A good, strong, and loving relationship needs to have the strength of two people coming together who are willing to protect each other in all phases of their relationship.

Life can crush bonds. A good relationship is based on trusting each other to help against the crush of daily life. Each partner can fill the cracks with love to gain the strength to stand against the forces of nature. When two people come together, they are strong and stand firm, but apart they are weak and fall down. In demanding times, we must rely on our friends to join us in standing strong against the crush of life.

The arch in love is a symbol of unity, perfection, renewal, hope, trust, and strength. The pillars of love are unique in design because together they can hold up a lot of weight. Take a bridge, for example. It would collapse with one pillar alone, but with many it can hold thousands of pounds. As a couple falls deeper and deeper in love, the bearing points of an arch are accomplished by each half joining to the other to form the arch. An arch is a good example of the unification of two people. The arch is not only for strength but a covering for protection. A safe place. With this concept, there is strength and a lasting relationship of trust and true love. One person cannot make a relationship strong. A strong relationship is made by two people standing together against the forces of nature.

27. THE LIGHTHOUSE

"Don't forget that maybe you are the lighthouse in someone's storm."

PARKER GROVE

What does it mean to be the light in times of darkness? When we find others troubled, we offer hope, encouragement, kindness, and compassion. In times where others are struggling, we offer a way to help them regain their glow.

We can also offer wisdom and guidance, or just sit with someone and be the presence they need. It may mean offering strength to those who are feeling a moment of weakness or a smile and joy to someone in random parts of our day. In the past, they likely helped your heart to glow even brighter from a kind word, encouragement, a smile given, or joy shared.

Sometimes we simply need to be still and show that nothing needs to be said until the time is right. Our goal should be to foster peace and show others the joy that is present. Forget about the past. Be there for them when they are most vulnerable.

It also means protecting your flame from being blown out so that you can be the light for others. In truth, beauty, and goodness, we are the beacon. In times of trial and struggle, it means illuminating what is wonderful.

Sometimes we can find it difficult to be the light, but when we focus on the divine, it becomes easier. It could mean loving someone despite their flaws, helping someone through a situation they don't know how to overcome, or empowering others to triumph over whatever they are facing.

I encourage you to reach out to someone you haven't spoken to in a long time and let them know you care, that they have value and worth. Let them know they are not forgotten. Radiate joy and celebrate the blessings that are present in life. Forgiveness is key, let the Lord pave the rest of the way.

28. KINDNESS

"One of the most important things you can do on this earth is to let people know they are not alone."

SHANNON ALDER

It's hard being someone's friend when they are depressed, but it is one of the kindest and noblest things one person can ever do for another. Life is sometimes beyond our understanding, but that doesn't mean we are helpless. It means that we try to the very end. You don't know what issues they are facing and, for all you know, your story could pale in comparison to what they are going through. The two of you are connected by one thing: you both suffer from the demon that rides your back every day, a demon that does not respond to questions, does not adhere to logic, and seems invincible to all attempts of reason.

But there is one way to deal with it; it's to realize that we are not alone. At some point in our lives, we would have done anything to have someone to tell us they were with us. I am terrified that someone else, someone I could possibly help, is stuck somewhere I know too well, and I would do everything within my power to get them out. I'm not being melodramatic by asking for help and nor do I expect someone to understand the complex chain of events that led me down that dark hole. After all, my traumatic experience is not one that I would ever wish upon anyone else.

When I am down that void, struggling, I want to know that if I reach out, I can feel someone else fighting to give me hope, to give me a push to keep at it. Even though you might not think it, everyone in the world needs you. Everyone who is down and fighting needs you, and you need them now more than ever. Fear nothing; failure is commonly found along the path to success. Reach out for help. Express your desire to assist others in time of need. You too will benefit. Your Lord is watching. Just remember, you're not alone.

29. BENEVOLENCE

"There are few who plant trees, under whose shades they do not expect to sit."

NELSON HENDERSON

It's not often that someone gives you something and wants nothing in return. It is the ultimate reciprocity, giving what is not owed or due to others. This unconditional kindness is the greatest gift you can bestow upon another. It is the true meaning of life. We all have unique gifts to offer to the world. Our reward may not be seen until we are gone, but the promise of a better tomorrow for someone else is truly gratifying.

As humans, we have an innate sense of morality. No matter what religion, race or color we are, certain qualities serve as the moral standard. We admire justice, bravery, honesty and compassion. We abhor those who demonstrate treachery, cruelty, or corruption. Moral standards are universal and one of the most important aspects of being human. It is adherence to good manners and respect for one another.

Being kind is a fundamental part of our being. It is engrained in our soul. Those who are kind to others make this world better for everyone involved. God is the One who provides for us, and He expects us to share generously. We are encouraged to be benevolent and unselfish with our possessions, with our time, and with our exemplary behavior toward others.

30. THE UNCOVERING

> *"Finding yourself is actually returning to yourself. An unlearning, an excavation, a remembering who you were before the world got its hands on you."*

EMILY MCDOWELL

Uncovering yourself is not how you go about your life. You are not astray. Your true self is right there, buried under cultural conditioning, other people's opinions, and inaccurate conclusions you drew as a child. They became your beliefs about who you are. Discovering yourself is returning to yourself. It is an unlearning, an excavation, remembering who you were before the world got its hands on you, a revealing of your soul before society judged you and shunned you.

The greatest and most important adventure of our lives is discovering who we really are. So many of us walk around either not knowing or listening to an awful inner critic that gives us all the wrong ideas about ourselves. This personal journey is one every individual will benefit from taking. It is a process that involves breaking down and shedding layers that do not serve us in our lives and don't reflect who we really are. It also involves a tremendous act of building up and recognizing who we want to be, then passionately going about fulfilling our unique destiny.

To uncover who we are and why we act the way we do, we have to know our own story. Being brave and willing to explore our past is an important steppingstone on the road to understanding ourselves and becoming who we want to be. To find ourselves, we must seek our sense of purpose. This means separating our point of view from other people's expectations of us. It means asking ourselves what our values are, what truly matters to us, and then following the principles we believe in.

Be kind to yourself. Embrace the person you are becoming. Learn to live with yourself. The best way to find yourself before life adapts you to an unfulfilling journey is to lose yourself in the service of others. Generosity can enhance one's sense of purpose, giving our lives more value and meaning. Stand tall with a purpose and don't allow the world to change you from what you really are: God's angel.

CHAPTER VII

HOPE

When we have hope, we create a vision for our future during times of uncertainty. A subtle light enters our world through a beacon of our soul. I will share parts of myself that can serve as a lighthouse for others amidst the storm called healing. Having ambition creates perseverance, instills a positive mindset, and inspires action toward achieving a better outcome. With the power of desire, anything is possible, just like how a beacon provides direction and reassurance during challenging times. In this chapter, you will be inspired to learn that hope lies in the path of righteousness and only through kindness will you be able to see the wisdom and guidance needed to dream of a beautiful tomorrow.

1. HOMESICK

*"I am homesick for a place I am not sure even exists.
One where my heart is full, and my soul understood."*

MELISSA COX

I find myself waking up with an indistinct ache deep inside my heart. I may not be sure what is missing, nor why I am hurting. It seems like it is fear, but I cannot identify a specific scenario that frightens me. Several things might be out of place in my life, but I have had this feeling occasionally over the years.

Too early in life, I realized life is short. The number of days in our life is not guaranteed. Perhaps these experiences affect I negatively and create fear and regret within me. When I feel this numbing sensation within, I believe there is something else missing. I try to put the feelings into vague words so the world can understand my pain, or maybe relate to the hurt.

I long for a feeling I've never had, one I don't even know I'd recognize if I did. I don't know where I am going, but I know I'm on my way, and I'm giving my whole self to this journey. I wanted to turn my life into art, my very existence into a poem. It might not always be easy, but it will always be beautiful.

Being homesick is a sign of how deeply rooted your connections are. Each moment away builds your strength, making the return all the more meaningful. Every day apart brings you closer to understanding the value of home, while teaching you that you carry pieces of it wherever you go. Stay strong—home is not just a place, it's the love that follows you in spirit, no matter where you are. Home is where you heart resides and where your soul rests.

2. THE MIRAGE

"I see you across the dunes as a distorted blurry image. Yet in that moment of desperation, I realized that like always you are merely a beautiful mirage."

MIHIKA DAVE

The desert has always remained a mystery—its formation and disappearance and its mysterious way of supporting life. A mirage is an optical illusion caused by atmospheric conditions, but those false perceptions can also be caused by an altered state of mind. A mirage can make something appear real or possible when it is not so. It may cause hallucinations, a dream that gives the appearance of fantasy.

While driving through Death Valley, California, I came across the Mesquite Flat Sand Dunes. The sea of sand with its shadowed ripples and stark, graceful curves grabbed my attention. With temperatures reaching a blistering 118 degrees, I was able to reach the top of the dune and back safely. It was an extreme experience, where plenty of water was essential. The beating sun showed no mercy, and my hat was vital to staying cool. I saw many mirages along the way, but I realized they were a reflection of my thoughts at the moment. They were of objects, places, and people who were on my mind at that time.

Like a mirage, individuals we hold dear to our hearts can also become apparitions. Have you ever had someone in my life who was the one beautiful soul you could never grasp? They were the one marvelous star that was too bright for you, the mirage you were desperately seeking and blindly following. Although their image might be a little blurry with all the time that has passed, you still see their face when you close your eyes. You can sense the touch of their hand even though you are merely imagining it. You knew it wouldn't last, but at that time they were exactly what you needed to survive. You needed to be loved and listened to. You needed them. But you are stronger now, so you thank them for loving you right when you needed them to. You thank them just the same for letting you go. You both knew it was never meant to last forever.

And still, our hearts will always hold each other's missing puzzle pieces. That hand that reached out and rescued the other when you were both drowning. You thank that person for keeping you alive long enough to understand what you were truly worth. You can always hope but never forget to fear your Lord. You trust that He has you in His care and He has the power to make even a mirage into a real-life possibility.

3. TEARS

"You may forget someone you laughed with, but you will never forget someone you cried with."

KHALIL GIBRAN

When we cry, our tears are an expression of distress, pain, and sorrow. This powerful side of our human experience also speaks of fear, pain, and grief. Tears are sacred. They are not the mark of weakness, but of power. There is something holy about the droplets that run down from our eyes. Tears speak the language of grief. They mark the places touched by unspeakable love. They materialize hope.

We do not forget those we cried with. We do not lose the memories we discovered with them. They last a lifetime. Even when we do everything we can to move forward, to find peace, the tears will remain in our memories. Those who were with us during this immensely painful moment in our life will also be remembered, either in a positive or negative way. Hope is attached to the tears of sorrow. With hope, the cries of the brokenhearted are heard.

We won't find ourselves crying with many people throughout our lives. We will chortle with many but lament with very few. We tend to laugh with people but will not open our wounds so easily. We will find ourselves in amusement and derision, but these moments can be easily forgotten. We tend to shed tears with only a few select individuals in our lives because they are important to us. They understand us. They comfort us. Unfortunately, they will also hurt us tremendously. It is for these reasons that they will never leave our memories.

Tears in the hope of pleasing your Lord is where we obtain our true comfort. Tears of brokenness and vulnerability can encounter us all. It is in these moments that we desire and dream of a better tomorrow. We want a future of certainty and become hopeful about what is best for us. God's grace will always shine on our path of hope and the steps to our destination will always unknowingly be built with the tears we shed.

4. SILENCE

> *"The silence you left me with was the loudest noise*
> *I've ever heard. So loud that it broke my heart."*

THELONIOUS MONK

Silence during hopeful moments represent the space where one waits for something to happen. This silence can be filled with doubt, longing, or even a fragile peace. Have you ever been heartbroken by the sound of silence? Does the silence in your narrative act as a barrier to reconciliation, or is it a necessary step towards eventual healing?

Deep down, you already knew their answer, but for some reason you wanted them to say it. And with every minute that passed, you felt your heart sinking lower into your stomach. During that last meeting, unbeknownst to you, they had already made up their mind. They waited for you to take your last sip before they decided to walk away. The cold air had yet to settle before the abrupt ending ensued.

The silence was deafening. With darkness pressing in, your broken heart and empty mind raced quietly. The sorrow and pain remained unknown to others as you treaded toward eternity. You waited and waited; for minutes, for hours, for days, but all you heard was silence. And with the absence of their words, you took it as an answer. Words may sting, but silence breaks the heart. Memories cloud the past because silence hurts more than truth. This is why the loudest silence always comes from the sound of a broken heart.

Silence is wisdom. The Lord wants us to remain silent unless we are connected to a good word. It's a way to avoid saying something we might regret later. Becoming aware of the tongue is a sign of fear and sincerity. Silence is the most beautiful form of music. It is the origin of life, the key to unlocking the secrets of our existence and possessing the forgotten and neglected treasure hidden within our being.

If you've experienced heartbreak, I hope you find the power to move on. I hope you see the good in others and continue to live a life of integrity and spiritual growth. With each passing day, I hope you forgive and seek your Lord's message. In the end, only the silence between you and your Lord will mend your broken heart. Until then, be patient, pray, and experience the magical world of silence.

5. HEALING

"It's such a colossal effort not to be haunted by what's lost, but to be enchanted by what was. I don't know how the heart withstands it."

JANDY NELSON

The heart can be underestimated. Its powers are enormous. It can bear the weight of many troubles and tribulations, and it can resist and hold up against pain, trauma, sadness, and grief. But remember that the heart *can* heal you.

Coping with the loss of someone or something you love is one of life's biggest challenges. Grief is a natural response to loss. It's the emotional suffering you feel when something or someone you love is taken away. Often, the pain of loss can feel overwhelming. You may experience all kinds of difficult and unexpected emotions, from shock or anger to disbelief, guilt, and profound sadness. The pain of grief can also disrupt your physical health, making it difficult to sleep, eat, or even think logically. These are normal reactions to loss. The more significant the deprivation, the more intense your grief will be. The heart can withstand loss. It may seem impossible, but the heart can recover even if it takes years.

What is utterly amazing about the heart is how it remembers. Even through pain and suffering, the heart records every detail of the loss. Healing happens gradually; it can't be forced or hurried. Whatever your grief experiences, it's important to be patient with yourself and allow the process to naturally unfold. It fills us with great delight knowing that the heart will never forget the past. We simply move forward.

The miracle of the heart is to listen to its wisdom and integrate a divinely inspired approach by fixing and realigning your broken soul. Our souls were designed to remain connected to our loved ones forever. They were designed to bring us the healing light from heaven to help us process loss with love and support. Just like our ancestors did before us, we can learn how to reconnect and heal our grief through our hearts. In doing so, our hope for better a day becomes reality.

6. SORROW

*"Be polite in your sadness, classy in your
pain, and grateful amidst your tears."*

ZAHRA ANWER

As difficult as it may seem, be humble when going through life's challenges. You will endure sadness and pain. You will cry and suffer gratefully. You must look beyond the need for self-gratification, and further still, beyond the need to acquire possessions. Life is but an impermanent pause on the way to life everlasting. This world is but a transient moment, sometimes overflowing with moments of boundless joy and happiness, but at other times filled with sadness, sorrow, and despair. This is the nature of life, of the human condition.

You will face triumph and defeat. You will encounter love and heartbreak. You will experience joy and sorrow. You will come up against failure and success. You will run into fatigue and repose, and you will confront pleasure and pain. But every moment in your life has an ending. Appreciating these fleeting moments makes life more meaningful.

When the surges of deep sadness come and bring tears to your eyes, that's when you know it's real. The people you grow up with, meet and spend time with; your friends and enemies; your family and coworkers; your soulmate and children… none of them will be with you forever. Love and forgive. Learn and be grateful as these people mold you into the person you will one day become. Misery, like jubilation, is a gift from your Lord. It will last only for a little while and then depart, carrying with it the details of its visit. Be hopeful in every phase of your life because everything is temporary.

7. DREAM CATCHER

"Dream bigger than the stars, deeper than the sea, higher than the mountains."

PENELOPE PEWTER

Dreams are part of our human life. We dream as we sleep, as we walk, and as we rest. Most of us believe dreams occur for a reason and do come true. Moreover, we believe that dreams are magical and powerful. To protect our dreams from bad ones and catch the peaceful ones, the ancestors created something called the dreamcatcher.

You can be someone's dreamcatcher, their shelter in the night. You can be their protector from fright. As if the two of your minds were entwined, you catch theirs and they catch yours. Be the hope for the less fortunate. Through your words, you can make someone's dreams come true. Dreams are a way for the soul to travel freely through the past and future, unconstrained by the material world. The real world and the unseen world are created by your Lord. The greatest of dreams is the nearness to God in this life and the next.

The dreamcatcher reminds us how important the dream world has been to people throughout time. Dreams have provided medicine men, shamans, and prophets a portal to another realm. Even though today most of us focus on the physiology of the dream state, we can still appreciate the power of our nightly visits to that other world.

8. FRAGILE

"Look at everything as if you were seeing it either for the first time for the last time."

BETTY SMITH

Everything we see will one day change. Everything has an ending. One day, everything we took for granted will be gone. The first time you see something, you will never see it the same way again. It is a reminder to always appreciate what you have at that moment in time. Seeing something for the last time gives you a sense of appreciation for the hidden beauty it always concealed from you. Nothing remains constant in life; everything changes. Some things will come back while some things will be gone forever.

Every moment in time is unique and a blessing, a period that will never be seen again. In the blink of an eye, these magical junctures will leave us all. When we look around at the people and objects that surround us, when we see them as if it was our first or last time, it will give us the true meaning of existence. Life is truly short; everything can change in a split second. So, when you look at your watch or that clock, remember that it represents time, and life is the limited amount of time we get on this earth. As time passes, our life progresses, and as easily as the clock can suddenly come to a stop, the same goes for our fragile life.

Always be hopeful for what you have now and what your Lord can provide for you. Aspire to have a vision where you are always thankful. Your desire for goodness outweighs the greed and wastefulness of time. Be thankful, for another blessed day is not only a belief but a way of life. Show gratitude every day, for nothing is promised. Life is short, but hope can last for eternity.

9. DECAY

> *"Some day the earth will weep, she will beg for her life, she will cry with tears of blood. You will make a choice, if you will help her or let her die, and when she dies, you too will die."*

BRULE LAKOTA

One day, the place we call home will no longer exist. Our residence will be taken away from us. Our habitation will be destroyed. One day, our abode, our nest, our origin will be gone forever. There is no other planet known to be capable of supporting life, and those that possibly can are incredibly far away. We have no other options. There are no alternatives.

We have a choice. We can either help the earth slowly recover or let the destruction continue. Our planet cannot continue if we do not take responsibility for change. We must act now before it's too late.

I urge you to change your habits. Our earth is slowly dying. From deforestation to pollution, there is only so much she can take. Overpopulation and overconsumption are slowly deteriorating our planet. Our climate is getting worse, and our natural resources are dwindling. Our ecosystems are being altered along with water degradation. We must make changes now.

While our earth faces many threats, there is reason to be hopeful for the planet's future. We must treat it as a shared asset capable of sustaining life far into the future. Having a planet-minded passion is a wonderful way to look forward with a sense of hope through meaningful connections. We can believe we have time, that we have tomorrow. We can assume that things will get better and unknowingly cause more harm. Truth is, our planet is slowly dying. With each passing day, it is weakening. Its precious riches are diminishing. And when she finally takes her last breath, we too will perish.

10. ASPIRATION

"Remember that hope is a good thing, maybe the best of things, and no good thing ever dies."

STEPHEN KING

Hope is a feeling of expectation and desire for a certain thing to happen. It is a feeling of trust. We expect a positive outcome with respect to events and circumstances in our life or the world at large. We like to be confident and cherish our desires with anticipation. But life can be beautiful and sometimes harsh. It's in these moments of vulnerability that we hold hope to a higher standard.

Have you ever felt fearless one day and lost and scared the next? The hardest part of going through tough times is not losing hope. That's why I hope you see things that startle you. I hope you live a life you're proud of. I hope you feel things you never felt before. I hope you meet people with different points of view. If you find that you're not, I hope you have the strength to start all over again. Cold, gray, and harsh situations might knock you down some days, but you're never a prisoner so long as you have hope.

We all have the hope for something better, hope for the future, hope to keep our heads up when things aren't going well. Once hope is lost, there is no middle ground. One may argue that one can simply accept things and move on, but if you can't win something, you've lost it.

Hope doesn't mean being totally ignorant and believing things will be dreamlike. It means knowing there is a capacity for things to change, to be better, and with this hope, one can use their abilities to work toward that. I hope this book becomes an inspiration to your ambitions and wishes.

11. THE MAGICIAN

> *"The syntactical nature of reality, the real secret of magic, is that the world is made of words. And if you know the words that the world is made of, you can make it whatever you wish."*

TERENCE MCKENNA

Words can shed some interesting light on the way language shapes our experience of the world if we interpret it a little differently. We can play with the structure of the world as processed through concepts simply by altering those very notions. The moment we start to use words, we are dealing with the conceptual world. We are mediating and processing reality through concepts and language. The meanings of the words are crucially important; they not only shape our perception but can potentially give us the power to modify our perception and the world we experience at will.

We are encouraged to explore the world of imagination, which is the essence and vitality of human life, and reject any authority imposed upon us from the outside. We should never underestimate words as their strength is strung together by our ability to wield them. Words are inexhaustible because they can both inflict pain and remedy it.

As a writer and author, it means I am a magician. I can cast powerful spells over the world by spelling words into existence. I can change the way people think, feel, and act. That's my ability as a poet, speaker, artist, and storyteller. It is my gift to influence others, to create the unexpected, to change the way people see and understand the world.

The next time you write, remember that you aren't merely spelling words. You are casting spells. So, embrace words and their power. Read, write, tell stories, and flaunt your magic. Be a magician because you never know who you will inspire and what impact your words will have on them. You might be the hope for someone looking for magic.

12. THE PRICE

*"The price of anything is the amount
of life you exchange for it."*

HENRY DAVID THOREAU

We often overlook the concept of time as life. We can grasp the concept well when it comes to other exchanges, but we seem to struggle when we put life and time together. Money is a commodity that is remarkably similar to time. There's only so much of it at our disposal. Once we spend it, it's gone, and we want to make fair exchanges with it. We strive to get value for our money spent because its limit is tied with time.

When it comes to the larger picture, we tend to either miss this truth or forget its veracity. There's nothing we can do in life that doesn't require this exchange. It's inescapable. Some believe they can escape the reality that no matter what we're doing, we're in the process of exchanging.

The biggest difference between money and time is that time cannot be replenished. We can always work more hours; We can make more investments or borrow money, but there's no way to acquire more time. Each one of us is allotted twenty-four hours each day that we can spend as we choose, but we cannot replenish it.

Time might be just an illusion, but its role in life is important. It helps everything and everyone move on. Our perception is that we all have the same amount of time to prioritize what is most important to us and we have the right to manage it the way we see fit. Thank your loved ones for their time and give yours to those who are worthy. Remember that time takes all whether you want it to or not, and in the end, there is only darkness. Sometimes we find others in that darkness, and sometimes we lose them there.

Nothing in the world can replace your time, life, choices, and actions. So next time someone wants you to do something; to be with them, or you're thinking of buying a bigger item, think about the amount of life you're paying for it and decide if it's truly worth it.

13. TRANSFORMATION

"If you only read the books that everyone else is reading, you can only think what everyone else is thinking."

HARUKI MURAKAMI

Do you like to read books? I spend my days and nights turning the pages to understand the plot. I imagine the next move, the next course of action. Do you read the same books as your friends? Or do you enjoy reading something more complex?

I want you to be different. Don't be afraid to sway from others who are the same. You may be considered an outsider or feel out of place, but you will benefit greatly. If we're reading what everyone else is reading, it's harder to think differently about problems, decisions, or life. You become boring, unimaginative, and lack the capacity to entertain innovative ideas. Maybe you've found yourself reading this inspirational book because that last non-fiction book you read was not motivating.

We have an obligation to make things beautiful—not to leave the world uglier than we found it; To empty the oceans, and not to leave our problems for the next generation. We have an obligation to clean up after ourselves and not leave our children with a world we've messed up, shortchanged, and crippled.

I hope you are inspired by the stories you read and by the words you decipher. I hope you discover meaning and purpose in your challenges. Your positive mindset can help you find hope even in dark times. Change is possible and starts with the awareness that the Lord is at work and has your best interest at heart.

14. ADMIRATION

"The admiration stage is a short-lived stage."

DARK NIGHT BEACON

Pleasurable contemplation, appreciation, respect, and approval are stages we go through. They are full of happiness, excitement, and joy. It's when we feel like we are on top of the world and with the one we desire. Nothing and no one can break your bond. Inevitably, it all gets too real, and you're forced to feel the possibility of losing something or someone so special. This brings up fear and conflict as we suffocate the very life we've become frighteningly attached to. That moment of your life flew past you in the blink of an eye.

The limerence phase is marked by a near-obsessive infatuation, strong attraction, and an often—overwhelming desire for reciprocation. This is the period of hope, not only for what the relationship is, but for what the relationship could one day be. The trouble is, when limerence expires, the real work begins. Love is forced to evolve into something more tenacious. The relationship is no longer sustained by only romantic attraction. When this obsession dies out, the couple sees the relationship in a more realistic light. Often the warning signs ignored early on remain as subtle but persistent seeds of contempt, a powerful threat to the bond.

I hope you experience a love that is limitless. Love in all its infinite glory is only experienced when it's not limited to sight. There is an innocence in admiration. It occurs in one who has not yet realized that they might one day be admired. I hope you admire those you respect so that it can inspire and encourage them, and they can recognize their own potential and become meritorious.

15. DRONES

"Your wings already exist; all you have to do is fly."

REUBEN WATSON

A drone is an unmanned aircraft. Drones are more formally known as unmanned aerial vehicles (UAVs) or unmanned aircraft systems. They can be used for photography, videography, surveillance, and search and rescue. Learning to fly one is not easy and can take many hours and flights to get comfortable. My hobby in drones has become a way for me to share my hopes and dreams with others through views from the cosmos.

My first drone flying experience was fascinating and gave me a bird's-eye view and perspective of the world around me. I soared above the clouds to capture magical photos and videos. These epic views gave me the inspiration to write and share with others about how hope can be motivated by almost anything that you find meaningful in your life.

Humans have always wished they could fly. They tried for years to invent special machines to fly. There are now many inventions that allow us to take to the skies; a drone is merely one of them. The desire to fly comes from an innate need to set ourselves free from all that holds us back. A drone allows us to go into the depths of heaven and observe our world in a way that only birds can see. Drones make our hikes to secluded locations exciting.

They give us joy to be able to see the world only seen in our dreams.

Do you think someone will someday invent wings for humans to use? Who knows what the future holds. For now, enjoy flying that drone and capturing beautiful moments of this magical world. Remember that time flies, but you are always the pilot. I hope all your flights in life are exhilarating and bring you happiness.

16. REMEMBRANCE

"And you write, because you want to say something. And you cry, because the pain is greater than you can bear. And you sleep, because you can't stay up alone. And that is how you are, because your heart isn't with you."

NIZAR QABBANI

When you lose someone you love, you also lose a part of yourself. You lose a part of your heart. This unique pain is an emptiness inside that lingers. You start to notice grief in other people. You get tired of waking up in the morning and realizing that whatever happened wasn't a nightmare. You sleep so that you are not alone.

Bad days happen no matter how long you have had to grieve and cope and process. It is okay to make time to miss someone. It is perfectly reasonable to take a step back and be sad. If it didn't matter, it wouldn't hurt in such an almighty manner. It is a blessing to know this pain, to have someone who made saying goodbye so impossibly hard. Sometimes, we don't even get a chance to say farewell as God makes the choice to return them to his grace and mercy. So, you cry because the pain never goes away.

When we mourn, we often forget that we did not just lose them; we lost a part of ourselves too. The person we could have been with and the future that we now don't get the chance to have. It is hard to be left behind. A part of you is buried with them. Everything changes in an instant you cannot control, and you are left to deal with the aftermath. You change and long to keep them alive. So, you write. It is in your words that you keep hope alive.

You want to remember the person you loved. You want to keep talking about them because staying silent about their lives seems worse than death. Staying silent is how some people choose to deal with loss, and that is okay. Everyone deals with it differently and there is no wrong way to do it. You choose to remember them because you know that when you grieve, it's because you got to love someone, and nothing can take that away. You learned it is okay that you are not the same person anymore, because you are forever grateful, blessed, and honored to have been a part of their life.

17. STRENGTH

"Greater is the one who sees the light at the end of the tunnel and keeps their eye on the light. Life is tough, but you are stronger."

RICH BARNES

Tunnels are a reminder to keep moving forward. Even when we can't see the light at the end, we trust that it's there. If we keep pushing through the darkness, we'll eventually come out on the other side. I want to remind you that the tunnel of hope is closer than you think. The burrow of your aspirations lies within. You just have to take a closer look.

When your troubles are growing and you sink into the darkness, it can be hard to find the motivation to keep going. We must embrace the darkness. Instead of avoiding the tough times; Lean into them. Ask yourself what you can learn from the experience. Look at challenges as opportunities for growth and transformation. When you find it difficult to see the big picture, focus on the small wins. Celebrate every victory, no matter how small. These little wins build momentum and keep us motivated.

Remember that it's easy to neglect ourselves when we're struggling, but self-care is essential to building resilience. Make time for the things that bring you joy, whether it's a hike up the mountains, listening to music, or spending time with your favorite book. Life is full of twists and turns, and getting lost in the darkness is easy. But with resilience and a plan of action, we can find our way toward the light. Remember, the light may be dim, but it's always there. So, keep moving forward, one step at a time, and you'll eventually reach a better place.

When looking back at the tunnel, I realize that all those events I endured made me who I am today. The tunnel is more important than the light because I experienced something new that can help someone else. All those little and significant moments in the tunnel are mosaics of myself.

The tunnel before the light is a little different. It is a battle you do not think you can get through, where death is being lived every day. Your strength begins when you push through to reach the light at the end of the tunnel. The beacon is waiting for you, have the courage to approach it and expand your mind. Your hopes will extend beyond the dark night.

18. THE WHISPER

"Goodbyes linger in the air, like a whisper of sadness."

D. L. HEATHER

I've always had trouble letting go. For as long as I can remember, I've held on to the past far too tightly, distracting me from the present. Saying goodbye has been especially difficult for me: the finality of it was far too much for my naïve mind to take. Once someone was gone, there could be no more conversations, no more gentle touches, no more time spent in each other's company. I can recall doing just about anything I could think of to be able to spend five more minutes with them. Yet, no matter how hard I fought, I would always end up having to say goodbye through tear-clouded eyes.

Leaving was tough, not only because the good times were over, but also because I knew they would always be held within my memory. I could replay the time I had over and over in my mind, yet I could never truly relive it. As time marches on, memory fades. What used to be recalled in vibrant color dulls with each passing year. However, with this, the wounds left by those who had bid farewell began to heal. Scars remained, but the pain subsided.

As I got wiser, I began to accept the small losses, but I was still unable to shrug off the greater issues. Have you ever lost someone dear to you? Did you wish you could say that you never blamed yourself, but to do so would be a lie? Love haunts us. It leaves remnants of itself in everything it touches. I know now that certain books, films, even clothes still bear the name of those who have already said their goodbyes. I cannot help but be reminded of those who have hurt me and those who had to leave far too soon, but I can choose not to let it affect me negatively. Life will always be filled with memories, both its ebbs and flows. It is a curse, yes, but it is also one of the greatest parts of living. Without the bad memories, how could we learn? Without the good, what would we be living for?

19. THE EDGE

> *"Come to the edge. We might fall. Come to the edge. It's too high.*
>
> *Come to the edge. And they came, And he pushed. And they flew."*

CHRISTOPHER LOGUE

I was speechless looking down at the graceful Merced River that flowed down the mighty Yosemite Falls. The plunge pool at the base is surrounded by dangerous jumbles of talus made even more treacherous by the high humidity and elevation. For those with a fear of heights, looking down would likely be terrifying. There is no fence, no handrails or yellow lines with a warning to be careful on its edges. One false step could lead to your death.

We need to get out of our comfort zone, to do things we thought impossible before and to take wings. How often have we stood by on the edge and not taken action because of the fear of failure? This is the dark cloud hanging over everyone's journey. Sure, transformation is terrifying, but the prospect of self-destruction is even worse. And yet, this is what makes our existence compelling, confronting physical and psychological fears in a strange new world where we are an underdog.

There is also the writer and their journey. At first, it is unshaped and unknown. All a writer possesses are a few stray ideas, images, and sensations. Those may excite the imagination, but there is the arduous work of brainstorming ideas, sorting through them, wrangling everything into a coherent narrative, and then trying to create imagery that encourages the reader's imagination. The hope is to captivate the mind of the attentive and to fascinate the thoughts of those who are appealing.

This process, confronting so many intangibles along with the very real possibility of failure, represents its own form of terror. Because as writers, whenever we are called to embark on a writing journey, we are enticed to the edge of what we know, the boundary of what we believe about ourselves as creatives, the fringe between creative ambition and the practical experience of surviving in the real world. The lure of the story pushes us over the edge. If we trust in the creative process, give ourselves over to the story, reach out to its characters, and believe they want us to tell that story, we will fly.

20. EMPTINESS

"Eventually, however, the denial turned into emptiness and my childhood ended."

FLOYD C. FORSBERG

When your childhood leaves you, your innocence goes with it. So too do your sentimental views of life and the innate process of development that only your parents could understand. Full of anticipation, simple, sweet delights are these childhood years, the most valuable of a lifetime. But the child hastens to leave its beautiful time and state and watches its own growth with impatient eyes.

I sought to return. The expectation of the future was disappointing. I was not in that free, powerful, and commanding state my imagination conjured. And the world, too, disappointed my hope. I found things that none of my teachers ever hinted to me. I beheld a universal system of compromise and conformity, and on a fatal day, I learned to compromise and conform.

I will never get my childhood back. The emptiness will always be there. That urge to be able to do the things I can no longer accomplish passes me by. And one day I realized the kid at heart staring at the mirror is gazing at an adult who was once so eager to grow up. I then understood that the day I felt uneasy about the future was the day I left my infancy behind. And before I know it, another birthday will pass me by.

Leaving behind the simplicity and innocence of childhood can feel like stepping away from a protective bubble. Yet, it's also a gateway to new opportunities, growth, and self-discovery. We can find hope in the unknown, in the freedom that comes with making our own choices, and in the possibility of redefining who we are. Remember that the best is yet to come – that we can find joy, purpose, and even playfulness in new ways as we grow.

21. THE PALM TREE

"May you never be too busy to stop and breathe under a palm tree."

UNKNOWN

Life is a precious gift that we often take for granted. It is important to take the time to pause and appreciate the simple moments in life, such as breathing under a palm tree. In today's fast-paced world, being busy is seen as a badge of honor. However, constantly being busy can lead to burnout and cause us to miss the beauty of life. It is important to be available for rest and relaxation in order to recharge and appreciate the world around us.

Breathing under a palm tree is a symbol of taking a pause and appreciating the beauty of nature. The gentle sway of the leaves, the warm sun on our skin, and the sound of the ocean waves in the distance can help us connect with our surroundings and find inner peace. During my trip to the beautiful palm tree fields in Mecca, California, my thoughts about life were triggered by the sway of the trees and the shadows of their fronds. A moment of silence was all it took for my imagination to yearn for nature's secrets and the reason we all seek serenity and contentment in a world that is fast-moving and absent-minded.

Life is about balance and finding time to slow down and treasure our surroundings. It is about admiring our society; Cherishing our planet. The world around us is just as important as achieving our goals and ambitions. Whether it's taking a walk in nature, meditating, or simply sitting under a palm tree and breathing, taking the time to connect with ourselves and our surroundings can have a profound impact on our well-being and happiness. So, take a moment to stroll under the palm trees and appreciate the simple beauty of life.

May all your trips be peaceful. May all your treks be full of joy. May all your excursions be with happiness. May your expeditions be full of delight. May your journey be full of exultation. Most importantly, may your voyage be safe and end with love. The next time you find yourself under a palm tree, think of God and how your qualities of righteousness, goodness, and abundance are all that is needed to enter God's temple forever.

22. THE UNIVERSE

"And, when you want something, all the universe conspires in helping you to achieve it."

PAULO COELHO

That's how the universe works, beautifully and magnificently. When you want something, you imagine it in your mind, you achieve it, and then you live it. We hold the universe in our hearts and minds. When we imagine something we aspire for, we have already achieved it in our thoughts and minds, and thus the universe makes it happen.

When you have the strongest desire for something, you make it happen. We fail to act on many occasions because we are not sure whether we want the outcome or not. This decision is greatly influenced by our subconscious, and we don't control it all the time. There always remains a gap between what we think we want and what we actually want. When you think about something passionately, you are linked with that thing. Your body starts to emit positive vibes about the thing you are asking for.

Thus, you ask the universe. The more you ask, the more you emit positive vibes, the more the universe around you gets to know about your aspirations. For your dream to come true, you must start believing it is already with you. You may want to achieve a goal, be with someone you love, wish others peace, gain something valuable, or even avoid misfortune. You must send a strong message to the universe about your desires, your passion, your affinity toward something. Though it sounds simple, it can be a difficult task. You must be strong and your similitude toward your wants must be even stronger. Only then will the universe rearrange itself for you.

You are the hope of the universe. You are the answer of the cosmos. You are the living being that cries out for peace, the light in the darkness of the infinite. When you hope, your foundation must be God, for the promises are found in Him. If God is not the source, it becomes a wishful thought. Hope is the beacon in the dark night. Its light shines through the storm of your soul, and when you allow God to anchor your hope, you will realize He's greater than any situation you will ever encounter.

23. MEMORY

> *"Sometimes you will never know the value of a moment until it becomes a memory."*
>
> DR. SEUSS

Only after we lose something does the true value of that thing come into focus. At the current moment, we don't really understand what we have. We must value our present before it becomes a memory. It is only when the moment becomes the past that we realize we could have invested more in it. You've lost many things in life, and one aspect of each loss is that you never knew its value until it was no longer there. Even when you know something or someone will be lost, you still can't mentally prepare yourself for the reality of when it becomes a memory.

Memory is one of the most admirable traits of human psychology. However, it has some negative aspects. For instance, if you have dark memories hidden inside you, they will bother you. But if you have some positive memories, you can live with them for the rest of your life. They are nothing less than treasures. Therefore, try to live every moment happily. If you can live some happy moments, you will have the happiest memories.

Most of us do not appreciate a juncture until it becomes a reminder. Give importance to every moment because there is a possibility that you will miss some of the best times of your life. It doesn't matter if those moments are small or big if you are spending them with your loved ones. Give significance to the moments that you are living now, or it will be too late to live your life happily and positively.

Being hopeful means consciously valuing and appreciating something or someone. You never know when that person or object will not be there again. Be grateful for all blessings, no matter how small. No matter what hardship you face today, know that someone in this world is facing a more difficult task. The things we take for granted in life may be the things someone else is praying for.

24. EPHEMERAL

*"I cried over beautiful things knowing
no beautiful thing lasts."*

CARL SANDBURG

Everything comes to an end. Everything in life is provisional. All things and situations are temporary. Happiness is fleeting. Enjoy your life today, because that happiness may not exist tomorrow. It is also true that dreadful things come to an end.

Imagine being insignificant and indispensable at the same time. That's how the world is. This is the paradox that we're all part of. We both matter and don't matter. We can change the future yet can't leave a deep enough mark for the universe to even notice.

No matter what you do, what you change, what you believe, it will all be over someday. How you interpret this paradox and how you use it to shape the things you do is what makes you the person you are. What you believe matters and doesn't matter, what you find significant and what you find trivial, and what you dedicate your life to defines the person you become.

You weep because you realize you can't have it forever. There is nothing strictly immortal, because everything that has a beginning will also have an ending. Whatever is of nature to arise, all that is of nature to cease. Every moment, in its essence and beauty, will eventually disappear. The world of experience and the world of fate will meet and separate.

Nothing in the universe, including the universe, lasts forever. If you're wise, you'll make the most of the time you have. If you want your life to matter, then you must decide that it does. No one else will decide that for you.

Nothing in this world stays the same; everything is in a constant state of change. Pleasurable conditions, favorable circumstances, our relationships with those we hold dear, our health and well-being—any sense of comfort and security we derive from these things is continually threatened by life's flux and uncertainty, and ultimately by death, the most profound change of all.

25. RISE

*"It doesn't matter how far you might rise.
At some point, you're bound to stumble."*

OPRAH WINFREY

Each one of us experiences setbacks in life. Some of us have mental scars to show for it, too. Sometimes we work hard for the things we genuinely believe in only for life to not go according to our plans. In these moments, you might feel like giving up. Perhaps it's just not worth the heartache to go after your dreams. These feelings of pain and doubt are normal, but they shouldn't stop you. In fact, when you realize you've hit rock bottom, there's only one way to go, and that's up. The process may be a difficult one and may even take away all your energy, but with strategy and willpower, it can surely be done.

When I witnessed the Rise Festival in Nevada, it brought me a sense of inspiration and hope. As darkness set in, I lit the lantern and watched it fly away. To me, it was a beacon of light in the darkness that delivered healing and harmony to a collective group. The experience reminded me of the adversity we all face. A prayer and wish rose in the air as thousands of lanterns covered the pitch-black desert background. A full moon was also on the horizon for added spiritual energy.

I want you to have hope, to release your pain and experience a new beginning. Rise to new levels of potential. Rise to greater heights. Rise to the occasion. Rise with all your might. To rise is to have no fear. To rise is to face adversity. So, light that lantern and let it go. As it climbs up to the cosmos, release all that has held you back. Let your dreams fly. Connect with the energy of the universe. Set your intentions. Feel the weight being released into that dark, brilliant sky. From dreams to loss, unique messages take flight and become brilliant flames, like tiny little suns rising above our heads.

For many, the *Rise* is an opportunity to let go of their past, of the demons that had stuck their claws into their soul and weighed them down with negativity. For others, it is an opportunity to take their sense of loss, fear, or sadness and replace it with hope.

26. SICKNESS

"The most expensive bed in the world is a sick bed."
STEVE JOBS

Health is a mysterious thing. When we feel well, we assume this is how we are supposed to be. We take feeling good for granted. When we get sick, it is often an all-encompassing experience. We are faced with at least a temporary loss of our health, our feeling good, and we don't like it at all.

Each day, we must acknowledge our gratitude for our good health. We need to do what we can to improve our health. The small choices—to eat a little less, to exercise a little more, to push ourselves a little further—may not seem important today, but I promise you, they will matter tomorrow. Health is one of God's greatest blessings. It is a fundamental right of every human being, which makes it a powerful source of guidance. A balanced mind, body, and soul is vital for anything the heart chooses.

We are all bound to go through an illness, ailment, disease, or malady at some point. No one is invincible. Not even the best medication in the world can relieve some dispositions. Remember that you can employ someone to drive a car for you; you can have someone make money for you; but you cannot have someone bear the sickness for you. Take care of yourself today, because tomorrow may be too late. Health is the greatest gift, and the best wealth one can have. Material things that are lost can be found, but there is one thing that can never be found when it is lost, and that is life.

27. INNER PEACE

> *"True happiness comes from having a sense of inner peace and contentment, which in turn must be achieved by cultivating altruism, love and compassion, and by eliminating anger, selfishness and greed."*

DALAI LAMA

Inner peace means equanimity, inner harmony, and the absence of disturbing or distracting thoughts. It means a peaceful mind that can stay calm and recollect in every situation. This state of mind confers tranquility and peace, inner harmony and balance, and the ability to remain calm, undisturbed, and in control of yourself, even in difficult and unpleasant situations. When life events are given meaning in a way that satisfies the heart and mind, we are at peace.

Inner peace is important not only while things move smoothly, but especially in times of trouble, difficulties, or danger. That's when it counts the most. Everyone desires inner peace, even if they are not aware of it. Few realize the importance and benefits of inner peace, and still fewer know it is a skill that can be learned.

Peace is understanding and contemplating the divine singularity of existence. Peace is tranquility attained by acknowledging one's true self and one's true purpose of living. I want you to go out and enjoy the tranquility of nature, the peaceful and relaxing natural environment. Perhaps for just a moment, you can make the pain go away or the stress subside. I want you to take your mind to the unknown and dream a life that you shall attain, God willing.

28. CONCLUSION

> *"Have you ever wept bitter tears because a
> wonderful story has come to an end?"*

MICHAEL ENDE

When this story comes to an end, and it will, we will have lost people along the way. Hearts will be broken everywhere. We will all, no doubt, be touched by loss. The only way to make this count is to forge a way of living that is better. Life will be different. The things we took for granted before will show themselves in splendor, like the blessings that were hiding in plain sight all along.

There comes a time in our lives when we have to say goodbye to people who authored the story together with us. A time in our lives when we have to say goodbye to the life we have lived. Reliance on God is a spiritual virtue and a major stage in the ascension toward God's proximity. But remember that all things have an ending, and every story has a conclusion.

If you have never cried because a beautiful tale was concluding and you had to detach yourself from a story line with which you shared so many experiences, close a chapter that contained so many memories, and depart from the hopes and fears of the story, then you won't comprehend the wonders and accounts of a text.

When life seems empty and meaningless because a chapter in your life is ending, have hope that a new chapter is on the horizon. Have faith that the Lord will provide you with a new paragraph and a new sentence. When your journey becomes the book of your dreams, only then will you realize the power of the Lord and His infinite grace.

29. THE SECRET

*"There are some secrets which do not
permit themselves to be told."*

EDGAR ALLAN POE

From the moment in early childhood when we learn to lie, we also learn to keep secrets about ourselves. Later in life, most of us learn to keep other people's secrets too. Sometimes it's better not to reveal all your secrets. You hope no one ever finds out about the things you have kept hidden. We keep our identity a secret. Why? Because life can operate efficiently without disruptions. But in the end, we are still a person, not just a disguise. We keep secrets about ourselves to maintain our own self-esteem and sense of self, especially when we're not comfortable with what the truth says about us.

What is that secret, you may ask? Once it's revealed, you'll wish you never found out, and once you find out, there is no escaping it. You will never be the same again once you know the secret. If you attempt to move, the unrevealed will find you. If you try to inform someone, the surreptitious could haunt you. The untold can never be coded. Secrecy is the ultimate realm of creativity; it can be infinitely changed and reworked, just like your imagination. Secrets provide a mysterious presence of calm, quiet authority and draw people to the unflappable confidence and unbreakable stoic demeanor.

The texts you read hold many secrets. The authors behind the words will convey the secrets if they are read carefully. If you want to know the truth, open a book. Between the lines, you'll find what you are looking for.

And when the secret is found, relish its beauty and allow someone else to find it on their own. Your perspective on secrecy will ultimately come down to your beliefs and goals. We are enamored with transparency and the suspicion of secrecy, but these two forces are not mutually exclusive, and the best cultures and personal strategies incorporate both. Were you able to observe the secrets of this book?

30. THE END

"Another year has come to an end."

DARK NIGHT BEACON

It's hard to believe that the year is nearing an end, and another year will have come and gone. It seems like only yesterday that we were still fixated on a year we never thought would end. We failed and succeeded in this year's adventure. We felt it would last a little longer. We failed and succeeded in past adventures. This is life; we triumph, we diminish, and we get back up and try again. This makes us human. We are programmed to be caring, have feelings, and to give love. The most challenging part is not what we have done but how we will grow from it.

How can we better ourselves without coming to terms with the advantages and the drawbacks in our lives, the actions we take and the decisions we make? Life is not perfect, and neither are we. That is why it is essential to take the time to decompress and try to be better and do better than we did yesterday. If you can improve in just one aspect of your life, consider that victorious. Soon, other facets of your life will follow you positive energy.

One day, you will figure out what your legacy is, what God planned for you to accomplish, but until that day, try to better yourself. You will still make mistakes, and that is okay because you are human. Strive to be better than you were yesterday. Be kind, stay humble, use your manners, and always try to be the best version of yourself.

Never lose yourself while trying to hold on to something that's not best for you. But on the contrary, don't give up on something or someone if it makes you who you are. We all could use a little more kindness in this world, and the only way we will find that is by starting with the one person we can control: ourselves.

I realize I have hurt people by my words or actions even though I didn't have ill intentions. To err is human, so I ask for forgiveness. My goal is to become a better person, a valuable friend, and an effective writer. I want you to reflect on your actions, emotions, and thoughts. Understanding why you act or feel a certain way is the first step toward positive change. I want you to respond thoughtfully rather than reacting impulsively. Most importantly, I want you to have hope in God. Only the Lord can provide a deep sense of comfort, purpose, and strength, especially during difficult times. A higher power will guide your life with love and wisdom, even when things seem uncertain or painful.

Upon reading this book, I wish you nothing but the best. I hope all your wishes, endeavors, and dreams come true. May you have joyful, bright, healthy, prosperous, and happy days ahead of you. May the beacon of the dark night provide the guidance you need to prosper in the person you've always hoped to become.

EPILOGUE

As the world progresses, we find ourselves on an ever-changing path. The journey we embarked on in these pages has brought us through trials and triumphs, moments of doubt, and bursts of inspiration. Through it all, we have learned that the strength we seek often lies within us, waiting to be discovered and nurtured.

The quotes shared in this book remind us that no matter how daunting our challenges may seem, we possess the power to overcome them. Each step forward, no matter how small, brings us closer to our dreams and aspirations. The people we meet, the lessons we learn, and the experiences we gather all contribute to the mosaic of our lives, making us stronger and more resilient.

Remember, life is not about waiting for the storm to pass but learning to dance in the rain. Embrace each moment, cherish the journey, and never lose sight of the light within you. The world is full of possibilities, and your potential is limitless.

As you close this book, may you carry its message in your heart. Let it be a beacon of hope, a source of strength, and a reminder that you can achieve greatness. The road ahead may be long and winding, but with determination and faith, you can reach your destination.

As the first light of dawn breaks through the clouds, I

stand on the mountaintop, breathing in the crisp, invigorating air. The journey that brought me here was filled with trials, growth, and moments of deep introspection. I faced my fears, embraced my true self, and discovered a strength I never knew I possessed.

Looking back on the path I have traveled, I feel a profound sense of gratitude for the people who supported me and the lessons I learned. Every step, every challenge led me to this moment of clarity and purpose. I found my voice, and with it, a newfound sense of direction.

But as I gaze at the horizon, I know my journey is far from over. The world stretches out before me, full of endless possibilities and new challenges to conquer. I have come so far, but there is still much more to discover, both within myself and in the world around me.

In the distance, the silhouette of another mountain range looms, calling to me with the promise of new adventures and greater heights to climb. I feel a thrill of anticipation. The lessons I have learned and the strength I have gained will be my guiding light as I embark on the next chapter of my life. With a heart full of hope and determination, I turn toward the rising sun, ready to embrace whatever lay ahead. The first book of my journey has ended, but a new story is just beginning. And so, with unwavering faith in myself and the path I am on, I take my first step toward the future, knowing that the best is yet to come.

Thank you for allowing these stories to be a part of your journey. Now, go forth and write your own inspiring tale. The world is waiting for your light to shine. You are the beacon in the dark night! Until next time, may peace be upon you.

ACKNOWLEDGEMENTS

This book is the culmination of a journey that would not have been possible without the support, encouragement, and love of many incredible individuals. First and foremost, I am profoundly grateful to my parents. Your unwavering belief in me and constant encouragement have been my bedrock. By instilling in me the values of perseverance and hard work, it is an honor to call you my mother and father. To my family, your constant support and understanding have been invaluable. To my friends, who have stood by me through good times and bad, your encouragement has been a beacon of light during challenging times. Thank you for your endless positivity and for always reminding me to keep pushing forward.

I am deeply indebted to my editor, whose insights and guidance have shaped this book into what it is today. Your patience, expertise, and attention to detail have been instrumental in this journey. Thank you for your keen eye for detail in transforming my manuscript into a polished and captivating work.

To the book cover designer, I thank you for your artistic expertise and your understanding of the genre and the book's target audience. I applaud you for creating a visually appealing cover that captures the essence of the content and resonates with the intended readership.

To the book interior designer, I appreciate your attention to detail in creating attractive pages to catch the reader's attention. Your hard work and experience were integral in producing a creative concept that complemented the tone and theme of this book.

To the countless mentors and teachers who have guided me along the way, your wisdom and knowledge have been the pillars upon which I have built my understanding and growth. Your impact on my life is immeasurable.

To the readers, thank you for opening your hearts to these words. It is my hope that this book inspires and empowers you to pursue your dreams and overcome any obstacles you may face. Thank you to everyone who has been a part of this journey, whether mentioned by name or not. Your support has been a source of strength and inspiration. This book is as much yours as it is mine.

Most importantly, I am deeply grateful to God for His guidance, strength, and inspiration though the journey of my tumultuous life. Without His blessings, this achievement of publishing a book would not have been possible. Thank you, Lord, for providing me with the wisdom, perseverance, and support needed to bring this work to fruition. All praise is due to God, Lord of all the worlds.

Thank you from the bottom of my heart.

With deepest gratitude,
Dark Night Beacon

www.ingramcontent.com/pod-product-compliance
Lightning Source LLC
Chambersburg PA
CBHW072004170726
47999CB00013B/81